MathFlare

Name: _______________________

Class: ___________

Teacher: _______________________

Introduction

As parents and educators, we recognize the pivotal role mathematics plays in shaping a child's academic journey and future success. Yet, the path to mathematical proficiency can often seem daunting, fraught with challenges and complexities. That's where the transformative power of MathFlare Workbooks shine through, illuminating the way forward with clarity, precision, and purpose.

Introducing MathFlare Workbooks – a beacon of guidance, a testament to excellence, and a catalyst for achievement. Crafted with meticulous care and expertise, MathFlare Workbooks stand as paragons of educational excellence, designed to nurture young minds, ignite a passion for learning, and develop a deep-rooted understanding of mathematical concepts.

Picture this: your child eagerly delves into the pages of Mathflare Workbook, greeted by a step-by-step guide illuminated with vivid examples that demystify complex mathematical concepts. With each turn of the page, they embark on a journey of discovery, encountering thoughtfully curated practice questions that reinforce learning and hone problem-solving skills. And when they unveil the answers to those very questions, a sense of accomplishment blossoms within them – a tangible reward for their hard work and dedication.

But MathFlare Workbooks are more than just tools for learning; they are pathways to comprehension, fostering a deep-seated understanding of mathematical concepts through a sequential, logical flow. From fundamental principles to advanced problem-solving strategies, every chapter builds upon the last, ensuring a robust foundation upon which future knowledge can be constructed.

As parents, we yearn for nothing more than to see our children thrive, to witness the spark of inspiration ignited within them as they conquer academic challenges with confidence and poise. MathFlare Workbooks serve as partners in this noble endeavor, offering not just practice questions, but the keys to unlocking a world of opportunity.

And for teachers, MathFlare Workbooks stand as invaluable allies in the quest to cultivate mathematical proficiency in the classroom. With answers readily available, instructors can focus on guiding and nurturing their students, confident in the knowledge that MathFlare Workbooks provide a solid framework upon which to build.

In the pages of MathFlare Workbooks, we find not just the promise of academic excellence, but the seeds of a brighter tomorrow. So let us embrace the power of mathematics, let us champion the journey of learning, and let us pave the way for a generation of young minds poised to shape the world. With MathFlare Workbooks as our guide, the possibilities are infinite, and the future, bright.

Table of Contents

MathFlare
MATH WORKBOOK
Grade 2
Step by Step Guide and Essential Practice with Answers
Addition Subtraction
Multiplication
Place Value and Expanded Notations
Geometry
MathFlare Publishing

MathFlare
MATH WORKBOOK
Grade 2-3
Step by Step Guide and Essential Practice with Answers
Addition Subtraction
Multiplication and Division
Place Value and Expanded Notations
Geometry
MathFlare Publishing

MathFlare
MATH WORKBOOK
Grade 3
Step by Step Guide and Essential Practice with Answers
Multiplication and Division
Decimals
Place Value and Expanded Notations
Fractions and Geometry
MathFlare Publishing

MathFlare
MATH WORKBOOK
Grade 1
Step by Step Guide and Essential Practice with Answers
Counting and Numbers
Addition and Subtraction
Place Value and Expanded Notations
Understanding Time
MathFlare Publishing

MathFlare
MATH WORKBOOK
Grade 1-2
Step by Step Guide and Essential Practice with Answers
Counting and Numbers
Addition and Subtraction
Place Value and Expanded Notations
Understanding Time
MathFlare Publishing

MathFlare
MATH WORKBOOK
Grade 3-4
Step by Step Guide and Essential Practice with Answers
Addition Subtraction
Multiplication Division
Place Value and Expanded Notations
Fractions and Geometry
MathFlare Publishing

MathFlare
MATH WORKBOOK
Grade 4
Step by Step Guide and Essential Practice with Answers
Addition Subtraction
Multiplication Division
Place Value and Expanded Notations
Fractions and Geometry
MathFlare Publishing

MathFlare
MATH WORKBOOK
Grade 4-5
Step by Step Guide and Essential Practice with Answers
Multiplication Division
Place Value and Expanded Notations
Fractions and Geometry
Unit Conversion
MathFlare Publishing

MathFlare
MATH WORKBOOK
5
Step by Step Guide and Essential Practice with Answers
Multiplication Division
Place Value and Expanded Notations
Fractions and Geometry
Unit Conversion
MathFlare Publishing

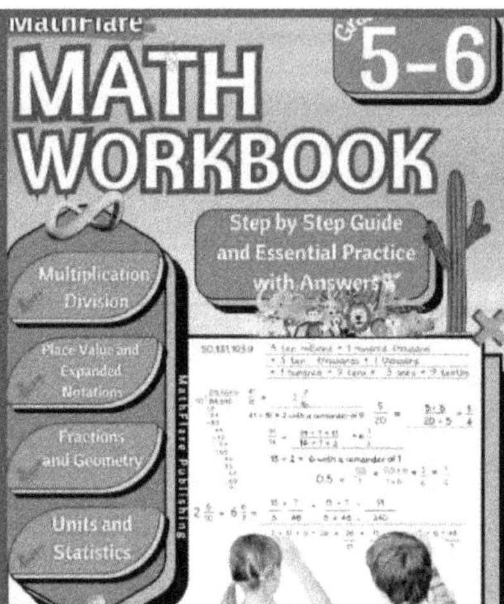
MathFlare
MATH WORKBOOK
5-6
Step by Step Guide and Essential Practice with Answers
Multiplication Division
Place Value and Expanded Notations
Fractions and Geometry
Units and Statistics
MathFlare Publishing

MathFlare
MATH WORKBOOK
6
Step by Step Guide and Essential Practice with Answers
Integers and Statistics
Arithmetic and Pre-Algebra
Fractions and Geometry
Ratio and Percentage
MathFlare Publishing

MathFlare
MATH WORKBOOK
6-7
Step by Step Guide and Essential Practice with Answers
Arithmetic and Pre-Algebra
Ratio, Percent Proportion
Geometry
Statistics
MathFlare Publishing

MathFlare
MATH WORKBOOK
7
Step by Step Guide and Essential Practice with Answers
Pre-Algebra
Ratio, Percent Proportion
Geometry
Statistics
MathFlare Publishing

MathFlare
MATH WORKBOOK
7-8
Step by Step Guide and Essential Practice with Answers
Pre-Algebra
Ratio, Percent Proportion
Geometry and Cartesian Plane
Statistics
MathFlare Publishing

MathFlare
MATH WORKBOOK
8-9
Step by Step Guide and Essential Practice with Answers
Pre-Algebra
Ratio, Proportion and Percentage
Linear Equations
Geometry and Cartesian Plane
MathFlare Publishing

MathFlare
MATH WORKBOOK
8
Step by Step Guide and Essential Practice with Answers
Pre-Algebra
Percentage
Linear Equations
Geometry
MathFlare Publishing

Multiplication and Division

Multiplication

Multiplication is an easy way of adding numbers together quickly. Instead of adding the same number repeatedly, we use multiplication to find the total much faster.

For instance, rather than adding 2 + 2 + 2 + 2 + 2, we can multiply 2 by 5 to get the same result: 2 x 5 = 10.

Here, the first number (2) is called the multiplicand, second number (5) is the multiplier. The answer we get, in this case, 10, is called the product.

Let's think of multiplication as repeated addition.

Take 2 x 5, for example. It means adding 2 together five times, which we can illustrate as: 2 + 2 + 2 + 2 + 2 = 10

Multiplication can also be visualized as groups of objects. Imagine we have 2 groups, each containing 5 oranges.

To find the total number of oranges, we multiply the number of groups (2) by the number of oranges in each group (5):

2 groups of 5 oranges = 10 oranges

Expressed as multiplication: 2 x 5 = 10

In summary, multiplication offers various ways to approach it: through repeated addition or by envisioning groups of objects. It's a powerful tool that makes solving math problems much quicker and more efficient!

We can also use the following table to quickly remember multiplication facts. The intersection of two points shows the product of two numbers.

For instance, the product of 5 x 6 = 30, or 6 x 5 = 30.

	1	2	3	4	5	6	7	8	9	10
1	1	2	3	4	5	6	7	8	9	10
2	2	4	6	8	10	12	14	16	18	20
3	3	6	9	12	15	18	21	24	27	30
4	4	8	12	16	20	24	28	32	36	40
5	5	10	15	20	25	30	35	40	45	50
6	6	12	18	24	30	36	42	48	54	60
7	7	14	21	28	35	42	49	56	63	70
8	8	16	24	32	40	48	56	64	72	80
9	9	18	27	36	45	54	63	72	81	90
10	10	20	30	40	50	60	70	80	90	100

Let's solve problems from exercises:

$$
\begin{array}{r}
1{,}202 \\
\times \quad\ 4 \\
\hline
4{,}808
\end{array}
\qquad
\begin{array}{r}
83 \\
\times\ 86 \\
\hline
498 \\
+664\ \ \\
\hline
7138
\end{array}
\qquad
\begin{array}{r}
552 \\
\times\ 908 \\
\hline
4416 \\
0000 \\
4968\ \ \\
\hline
501216
\end{array}
$$

Division

Division is like the opposite of multiplication. It's all about sharing or distributing items equally among a certain number of groups or people.

When we divide one number by another, we're essentially splitting a number into equal parts. We're figuring out how many groups of a certain size can be made from that number.

For instance, let's divide 20 by 4.

When we divide 20 by 4, we're essentially asking, "How many groups of size 4 can we make from 20?"

Now, there are several parts or terms involved in the division process:

- **Dividend:** This is the number being divided, which in this case, is 20.

- **Divisor:** This is the number we're dividing by, which is 4.

- **Quotient:** This is the answer we get after dividing. It tells us how many groups of divisors can be made from the dividend. In this case, the answer is 5.

So, when we divide 20 by 4, we found out that 5 groups of 4 can be made from 20.

Let's solve problems from exercises:

$$
\begin{array}{r}
4 \\
4\overline{)16} \\
-16 \\
\hline
0
\end{array}
\qquad
\begin{array}{r}
42 \\
12\overline{)504} \\
-48 \\
\hline
24 \\
-24 \\
\hline
0
\end{array}
\qquad
\begin{array}{r}
477 \\
6\overline{)2{,}862} \\
-24 \\
\hline
46 \\
-42 \\
\hline
42 \\
-42 \\
\hline
0
\end{array}
$$

Long Division with Remainders

Long division with remainders is a method used to divide larger numbers where the divisor doesn't evenly divide the dividend. Let's solve a problem:

$$
\begin{array}{r}
4{,}493 \ \text{R}5 \\
14\overline{)62{,}907} \\
56 \\
\hline
69 \\
-56 \\
\hline
130 \\
-126 \\
\hline
47 \\
-42 \\
\hline
5
\end{array}
$$

Using the Power of 10

Using the powers of 10, 100, and 1000 makes multiplying and dividing by these numbers very convenient. Let's illustrate with examples:

Multiplying by Powers of 10:

- To multiply a number by 10, simply move the decimal point one place to the right.

$$5 \times 10 = 50$$

- To multiply a number by 100, move the decimal point two places to the right.

$$5 \times 100 = 500$$

- To multiply a number by 1000, move the decimal point three places to the right.

$$5 \times 1000 = 5000.$$

Dividing by Powers of 10:

- To divide a number by 10, simply move the decimal point one place to the left.

$$50 \div 10 = 5$$

- To divide a number by 100, move the decimal point two places to the left.

$$500 \div 100 = 5$$

- To divide a number by 1000, move the decimal point three places to the left.

$$5000 \div 1000 = 5$$

Using the powers of 10, 100, and 1000 makes multiplying and dividing by these numbers simple and straightforward.

Multiplication and Division Word Problem

Anthony can run four laps in 1 hour. How many laps can Anthony run in 18 hours?

$$
\begin{array}{r}
4 \\
\times\,18 \\
\hline
+\,32 \\
+\,4 \\
\hline
=\,72
\end{array}
$$

1 hour 4 laps

how many laps can he run in 18 hours?

Anthony can run 72 laps in 18 hours

How many 12 cm pieces of rope can you cut from a rope that is 420 cm long?

$$\begin{array}{r} 35 \\ 12\overline{)520} \\ -36 \\ \hline 60 \\ -60 \\ \hline 0 \end{array}$$

35 pieces can be cut

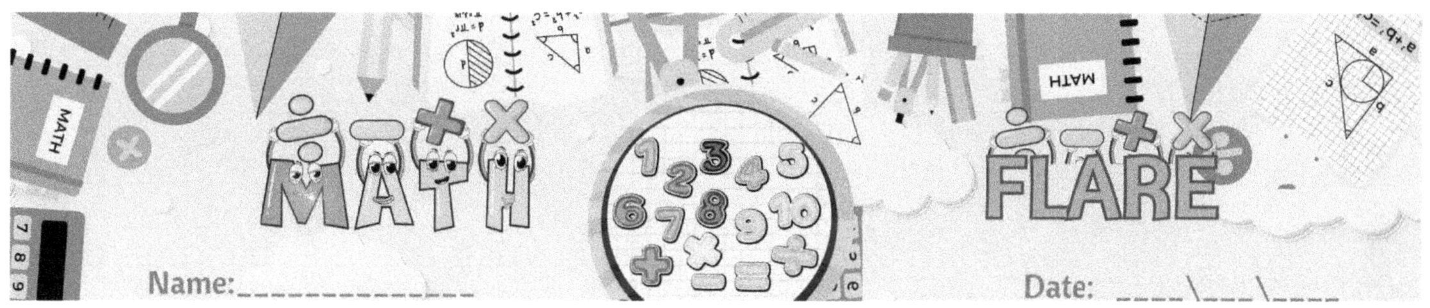

Multiplication: 4 x 1

Find the product.

1.
$$\begin{array}{r} 3{,}244 \\ \times\ \ \ \ \ 2 \\ \hline \end{array}$$

2.
$$\begin{array}{r} 1{,}311 \\ \times\ \ \ \ \ 2 \\ \hline \end{array}$$

3.
$$\begin{array}{r} 2{,}121 \\ \times\ \ \ \ \ 3 \\ \hline \end{array}$$

4.
$$\begin{array}{r} 3{,}214 \\ \times\ \ \ \ \ 2 \\ \hline \end{array}$$

5.
$$\begin{array}{r} 2{,}200 \\ \times\ \ \ \ \ 4 \\ \hline \end{array}$$

6.
$$\begin{array}{r} 1{,}931 \\ \times\ \ \ \ \ 1 \\ \hline \end{array}$$

7.
$$\begin{array}{r} 1{,}012 \\ \times\ \ \ \ \ 4 \\ \hline \end{array}$$

8.
$$\begin{array}{r} 2{,}113 \\ \times\ \ \ \ \ 3 \\ \hline \end{array}$$

9.
$$\begin{array}{r} 4{,}144 \\ \times\ \ \ \ \ 2 \\ \hline \end{array}$$

10.
$$\begin{array}{r} 3{,}023 \\ \times\ \ \ \ \ 3 \\ \hline \end{array}$$

11.
$$\begin{array}{r} 4{,}104 \\ \times\ \ \ \ \ 2 \\ \hline \end{array}$$

12.
$$\begin{array}{r} 1{,}021 \\ \times\ \ \ \ \ 3 \\ \hline \end{array}$$

13.
$$\begin{array}{r} 1{,}301 \\ \times\ \ \ \ \ 3 \\ \hline \end{array}$$

14.
$$\begin{array}{r} 1{,}212 \\ \times\ \ \ \ \ 2 \\ \hline \end{array}$$

15.
$$\begin{array}{r} 3{,}101 \\ \times\ \ \ \ \ 3 \\ \hline \end{array}$$

16.
$$\begin{array}{r} 2{,}021 \\ \times\ \ \ \ \ 4 \\ \hline \end{array}$$

17.
$$\begin{array}{r} 1{,}101 \\ \times\ \ \ \ \ 5 \\ \hline \end{array}$$

18.
$$\begin{array}{r} 6{,}485 \\ \times\ \ \ \ \ 1 \\ \hline \end{array}$$

19.
$$\begin{array}{r} 2{,}210 \\ \times\ \ \ \ \ 4 \\ \hline \end{array}$$

20.
$$\begin{array}{r} 2{,}110 \\ \times\ \ \ \ \ 3 \\ \hline \end{array}$$

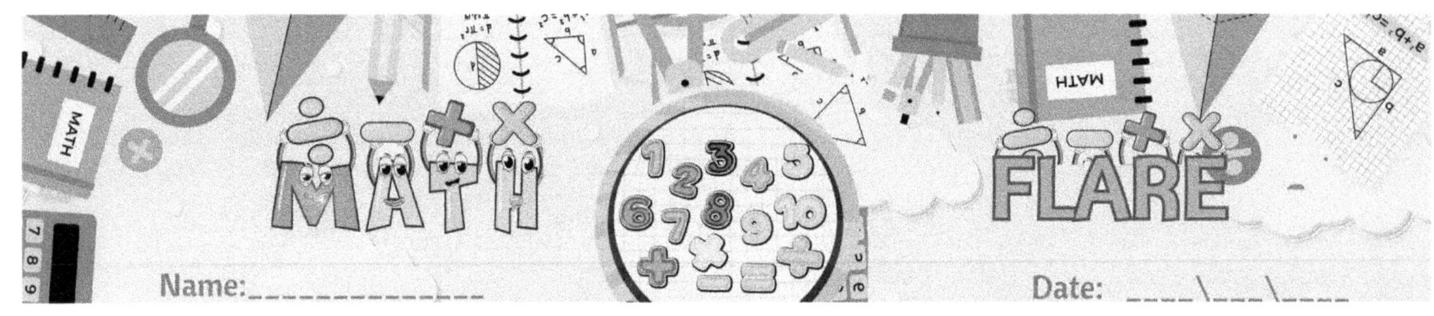

21. 1,214 $\times$ 2	22. 2,133 $\times$ 3	23. 3,332 $\times$ 2	24. 1,322 $\times$ 3
25. 2,131 $\times$ 3	26. 3,122 $\times$ 3	27. 1,012 $\times$ 2	28. 4,333 $\times$ 2
29. 1,210 $\times$ 4	30. 9,465 $\times$ 1	31. 3,302 $\times$ 3	32. 1,110 $\times$ 5
33. 2,130 $\times$ 3	34. 2,022 $\times$ 4	35. 3,103 $\times$ 3	36. 2,011 $\times$ 4
37. 8,801 $\times$ 1	38. 2,212 $\times$ 4	39. 1,121 $\times$ 4	40. 2,423 $\times$ 2

Multiplication (double Digit)

Find the product.

41.   81
    × 16
	42. 12
	    × 27
		43. 40
		    × 31
			44. 50
			    × 43

45.   37
    × 45
	46. 53
	    × 56
		47. 31
		    × 14
			48. 17
			    × 84

49.   60
    × 60
	50. 15
	    × 58
		51. 45
		    × 42
			52. 17
			    × 42

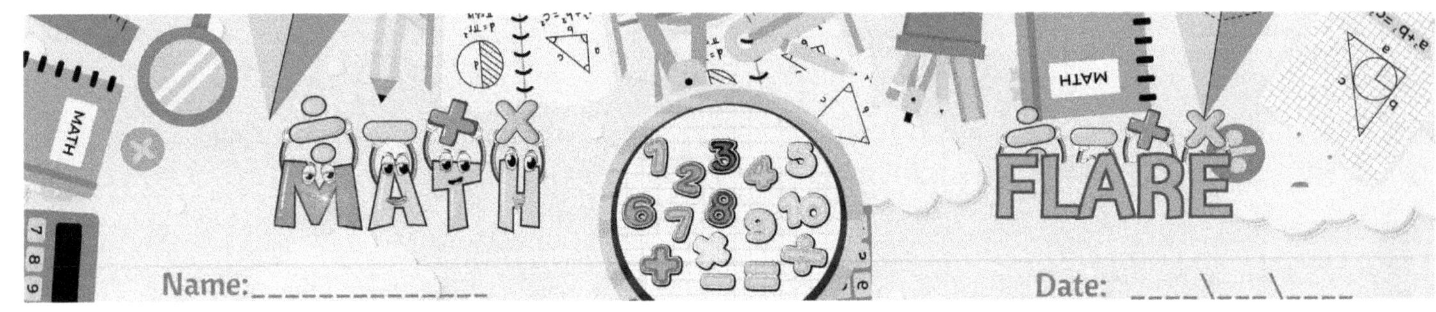

53. 63 × 48	54. 79 × 14	55. 11 × 15	56. 45 × 34
57. 87 × 38	58. 99 × 31	59. 76 × 42	60. 67 × 34
61. 75 × 61	62. 93 × 75	63. 49 × 76	64. 41 × 54
65. 66 × 44	66. 64 × 39	67. 41 × 82	68. 12 × 49

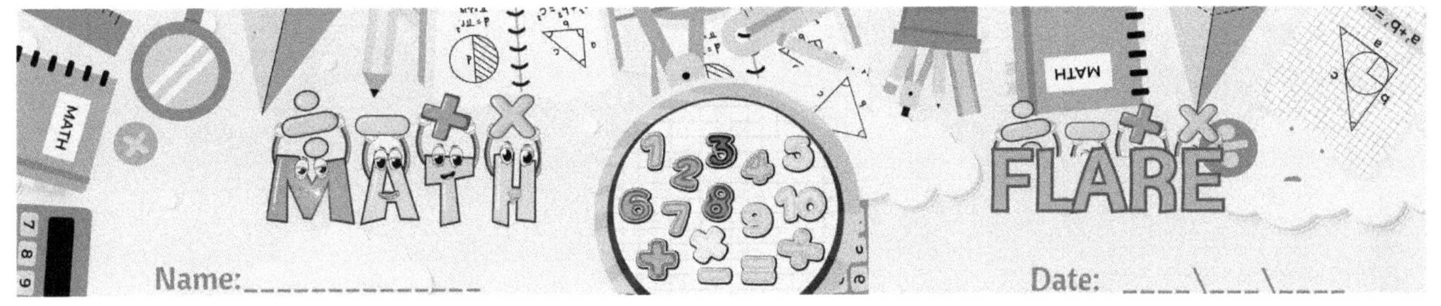

69. $\begin{array}{r} 97 \\ \times\ 70 \\ \hline \end{array}$	70. $\begin{array}{r} 63 \\ \times\ 92 \\ \hline \end{array}$	71. $\begin{array}{r} 50 \\ \times\ 46 \\ \hline \end{array}$	72. $\begin{array}{r} 42 \\ \times\ 32 \\ \hline \end{array}$
73. $\begin{array}{r} 99 \\ \times\ 29 \\ \hline \end{array}$	74. $\begin{array}{r} 68 \\ \times\ 92 \\ \hline \end{array}$	75. $\begin{array}{r} 14 \\ \times\ 86 \\ \hline \end{array}$	76. $\begin{array}{r} 17 \\ \times\ 29 \\ \hline \end{array}$
77. $\begin{array}{r} 93 \\ \times\ 81 \\ \hline \end{array}$	78. $\begin{array}{r} 82 \\ \times\ 83 \\ \hline \end{array}$	79. $\begin{array}{r} 48 \\ \times\ 41 \\ \hline \end{array}$	80. $\begin{array}{r} 91 \\ \times\ 86 \\ \hline \end{array}$
81. $\begin{array}{r} 17 \\ \times\ 35 \\ \hline \end{array}$	82. $\begin{array}{r} 47 \\ \times\ 66 \\ \hline \end{array}$	83. $\begin{array}{r} 50 \\ \times\ 16 \\ \hline \end{array}$	84. $\begin{array}{r} 92 \\ \times\ 15 \\ \hline \end{array}$

85. $\begin{array}{r} 35 \\ \times\ 60 \\ \hline \end{array}$	86. $\begin{array}{r} 32 \\ \times\ 17 \\ \hline \end{array}$	87. $\begin{array}{r} 78 \\ \times\ 74 \\ \hline \end{array}$	88. $\begin{array}{r} 82 \\ \times\ 39 \\ \hline \end{array}$
89. $\begin{array}{r} 29 \\ \times\ 71 \\ \hline \end{array}$	90. $\begin{array}{r} 76 \\ \times\ 30 \\ \hline \end{array}$	91. $\begin{array}{r} 18 \\ \times\ 48 \\ \hline \end{array}$	92. $\begin{array}{r} 50 \\ \times\ 79 \\ \hline \end{array}$
93. $\begin{array}{r} 37 \\ \times\ 46 \\ \hline \end{array}$	94. $\begin{array}{r} 45 \\ \times\ 60 \\ \hline \end{array}$	95. $\begin{array}{r} 11 \\ \times\ 66 \\ \hline \end{array}$	96. $\begin{array}{r} 78 \\ \times\ 76 \\ \hline \end{array}$
97. $\begin{array}{r} 85 \\ \times\ 25 \\ \hline \end{array}$	98. $\begin{array}{r} 99 \\ \times\ 76 \\ \hline \end{array}$	99. $\begin{array}{r} 82 \\ \times\ 92 \\ \hline \end{array}$	100. $\begin{array}{r} 37 \\ \times\ 64 \\ \hline \end{array}$

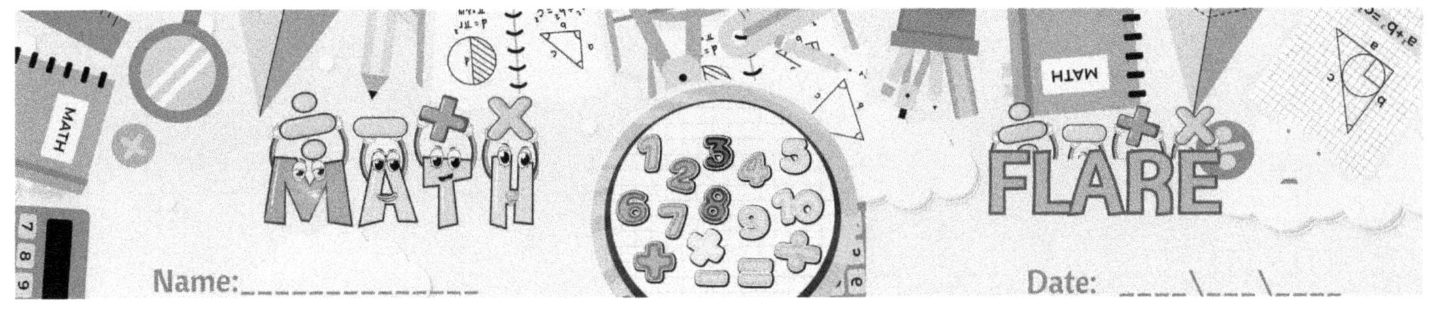

101. 67
× 53

102. 63
× 11

103. 50
× 29

104. 97
× 53

105. 64
× 76

106. 65
× 71

107. 78
× 68

108. 84
× 67

109. 39
× 14

110. 70
× 42

111. 15
× 17

112. 58
× 65

113. 38
× 12

114. 88
× 67

115. 39
× 52

116. 88
× 82

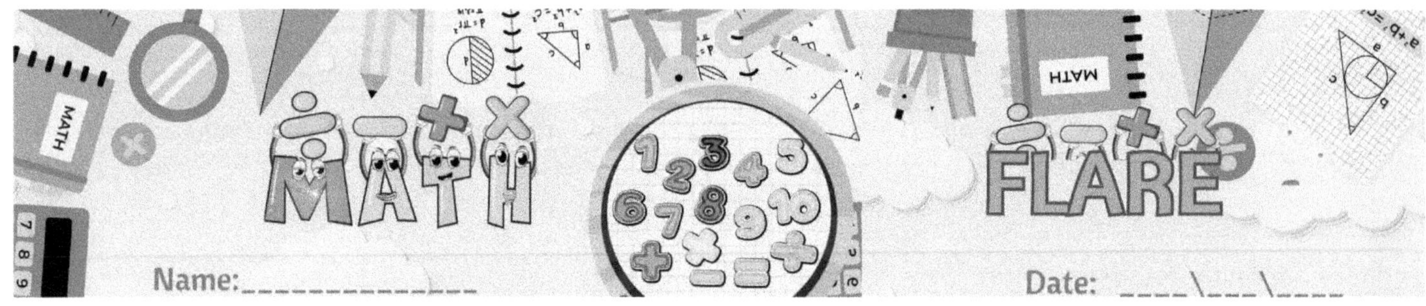

Multiplication (3 Digit)

Find the product.

117. 928
    × 536

118. 805
    × 964

119. 260
    × 362

120. 959
    × 268

121. 620
    × 559

122. 643
    × 345

123. 113
    × 162

124. 977
    × 276

125. 403
    × 423

126. 474
    × 787

127. 325
    × 949

128. 590
    × 610

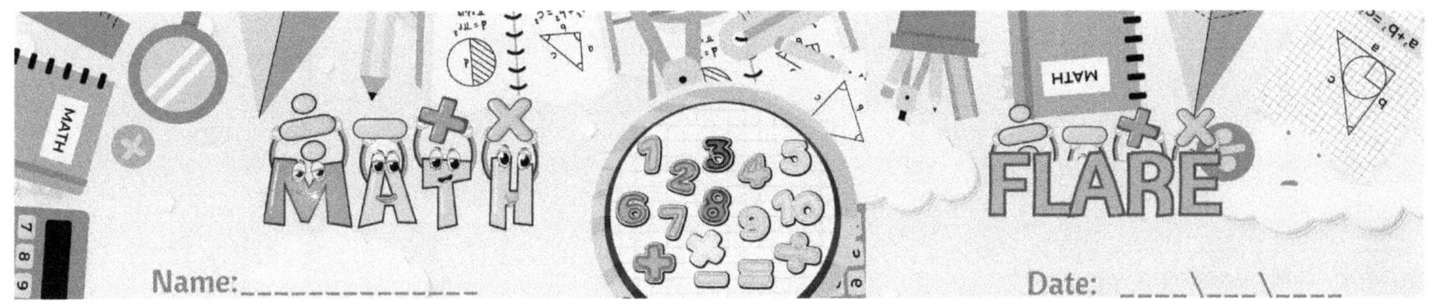

129. $\begin{array}{r} 950 \\ \times\ 982 \\ \hline \end{array}$	130. $\begin{array}{r} 724 \\ \times\ 481 \\ \hline \end{array}$	131. $\begin{array}{r} 400 \\ \times\ 404 \\ \hline \end{array}$	132. $\begin{array}{r} 243 \\ \times\ 221 \\ \hline \end{array}$
133. $\begin{array}{r} 881 \\ \times\ 823 \\ \hline \end{array}$	134. $\begin{array}{r} 791 \\ \times\ 352 \\ \hline \end{array}$	135. $\begin{array}{r} 876 \\ \times\ 884 \\ \hline \end{array}$	136. $\begin{array}{r} 512 \\ \times\ 130 \\ \hline \end{array}$
137. $\begin{array}{r} 178 \\ \times\ 538 \\ \hline \end{array}$	138. $\begin{array}{r} 801 \\ \times\ 592 \\ \hline \end{array}$	139. $\begin{array}{r} 523 \\ \times\ 344 \\ \hline \end{array}$	140. $\begin{array}{r} 644 \\ \times\ 321 \\ \hline \end{array}$

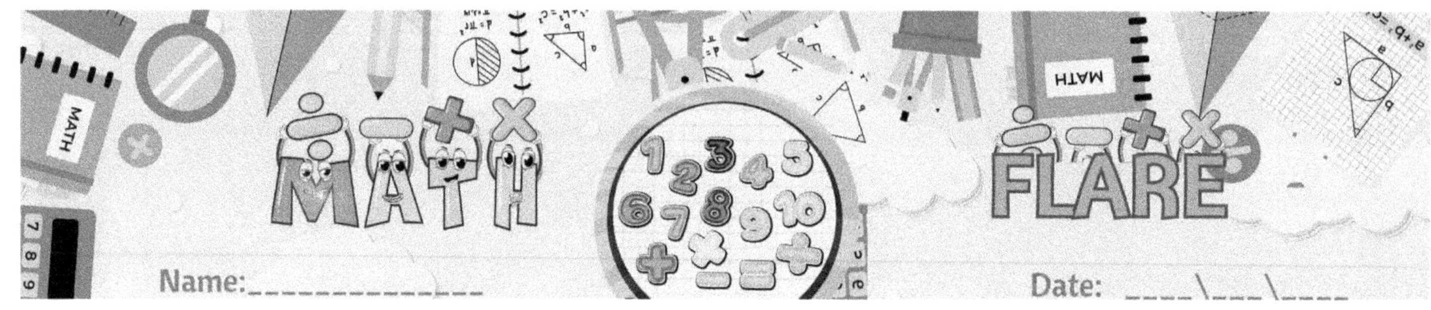

141. $\begin{array}{r}143\\ \times\ 711\\\hline\end{array}$	142. $\begin{array}{r}375\\ \times\ 970\\\hline\end{array}$	143. $\begin{array}{r}150\\ \times\ 199\\\hline\end{array}$	144. $\begin{array}{r}604\\ \times\ 977\\\hline\end{array}$
145. $\begin{array}{r}945\\ \times\ 295\\\hline\end{array}$	146. $\begin{array}{r}114\\ \times\ 276\\\hline\end{array}$	147. $\begin{array}{r}637\\ \times\ 579\\\hline\end{array}$	148. $\begin{array}{r}867\\ \times\ 316\\\hline\end{array}$
149. $\begin{array}{r}416\\ \times\ 523\\\hline\end{array}$	150. $\begin{array}{r}462\\ \times\ 289\\\hline\end{array}$	151. $\begin{array}{r}370\\ \times\ 725\\\hline\end{array}$	152. $\begin{array}{r}399\\ \times\ 518\\\hline\end{array}$

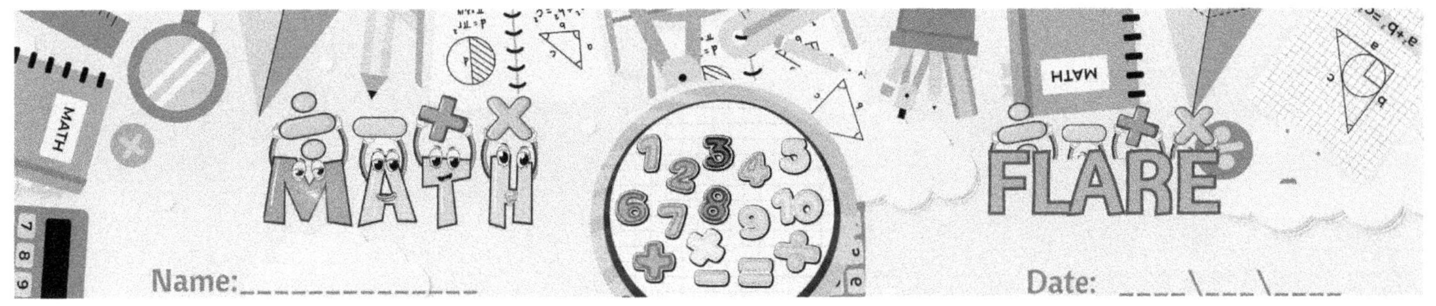

153.	154.	155.	156.
910 × 445	709 × 787	249 × 997	187 × 706

157.	158.	159.	160.
438 × 503	438 × 688	129 × 272	171 × 783

161.	162.	163.	164.
319 × 813	406 × 681	870 × 336	492 × 598

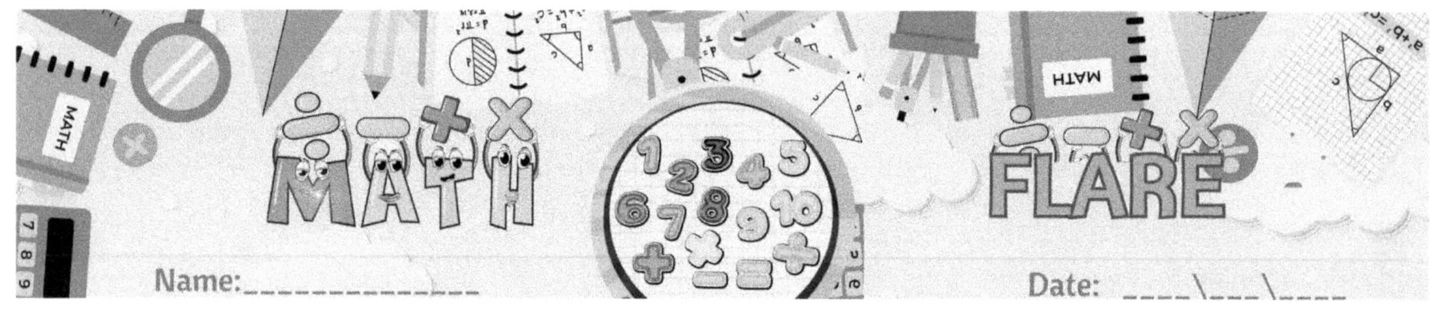

165. $\begin{array}{r} 669 \\ \times\ 584 \\ \hline \end{array}$	166. $\begin{array}{r} 276 \\ \times\ 100 \\ \hline \end{array}$	167. $\begin{array}{r} 880 \\ \times\ 455 \\ \hline \end{array}$	168. $\begin{array}{r} 951 \\ \times\ 417 \\ \hline \end{array}$
169. $\begin{array}{r} 413 \\ \times\ 855 \\ \hline \end{array}$	170. $\begin{array}{r} 160 \\ \times\ 704 \\ \hline \end{array}$	171. $\begin{array}{r} 488 \\ \times\ 817 \\ \hline \end{array}$	172. $\begin{array}{r} 829 \\ \times\ 947 \\ \hline \end{array}$
173. $\begin{array}{r} 207 \\ \times\ 407 \\ \hline \end{array}$	174. $\begin{array}{r} 837 \\ \times\ 234 \\ \hline \end{array}$	175. $\begin{array}{r} 241 \\ \times\ 279 \\ \hline \end{array}$	176. $\begin{array}{r} 287 \\ \times\ 244 \\ \hline \end{array}$

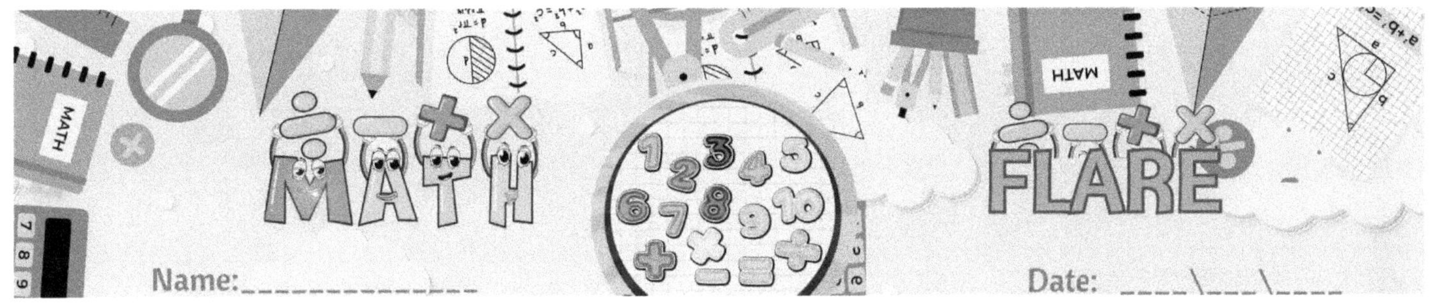

177. $\begin{array}{r} 451 \\ \times\ 679 \end{array}$	178. $\begin{array}{r} 969 \\ \times\ 556 \end{array}$	179. $\begin{array}{r} 419 \\ \times\ 716 \end{array}$	180. $\begin{array}{r} 648 \\ \times\ 674 \end{array}$
181. $\begin{array}{r} 952 \\ \times\ 211 \end{array}$	182. $\begin{array}{r} 217 \\ \times\ 664 \end{array}$	183. $\begin{array}{r} 822 \\ \times\ 187 \end{array}$	184. $\begin{array}{r} 825 \\ \times\ 982 \end{array}$
185. $\begin{array}{r} 551 \\ \times\ 121 \end{array}$	186. $\begin{array}{r} 375 \\ \times\ 273 \end{array}$	187. $\begin{array}{r} 212 \\ \times\ 466 \end{array}$	188. $\begin{array}{r} 395 \\ \times\ 501 \end{array}$

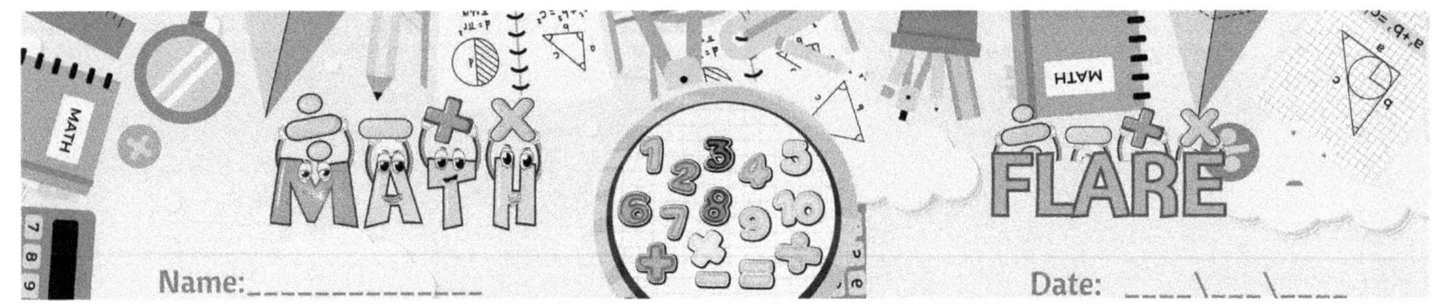

189. 983×458	190. 574×563	191. 498×358	192. 458×491
193. 397×131	194. 648×301	195. 485×495	196. 996×695
197. 308×484	198. 751×377	199. 699×265	200. 225×120

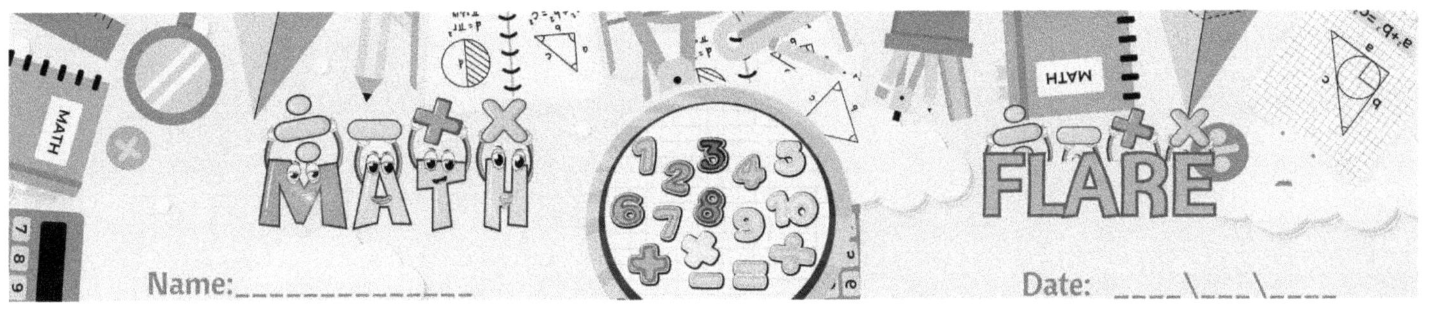

201.   581
   × 854

202.   682
   × 220

203.   903
   × 115

204.   132
   × 984

205.   384
   × 568

206.   571
   × 960

207.   242
   × 185

208.   277
   × 694

209.   752
   × 726

210.   367
   × 790

211.   539
   × 624

212.   597
   × 156

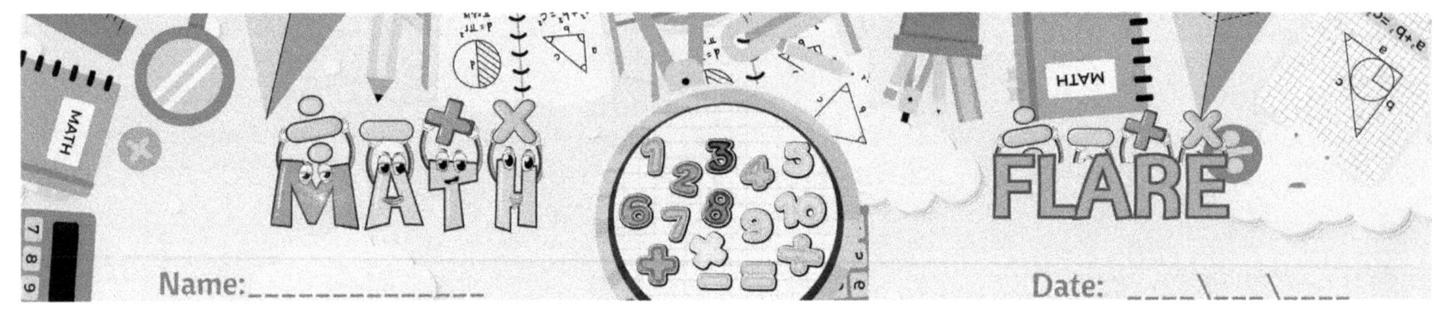

213. 124 × 679

214. 964 × 727

215. 714 × 117

216. 801 × 818

217. 333 × 554

218. 981 × 643

219. 675 × 338

220. 587 × 382

221. 998 × 663

222. 916 × 916

223. 923 × 136

224. 553 × 223

Long Division: Remainders

Find the quotient.

225.

18) 3,425

226.

4) 8,088

227.

17) 3,415

228.

13) 8,606

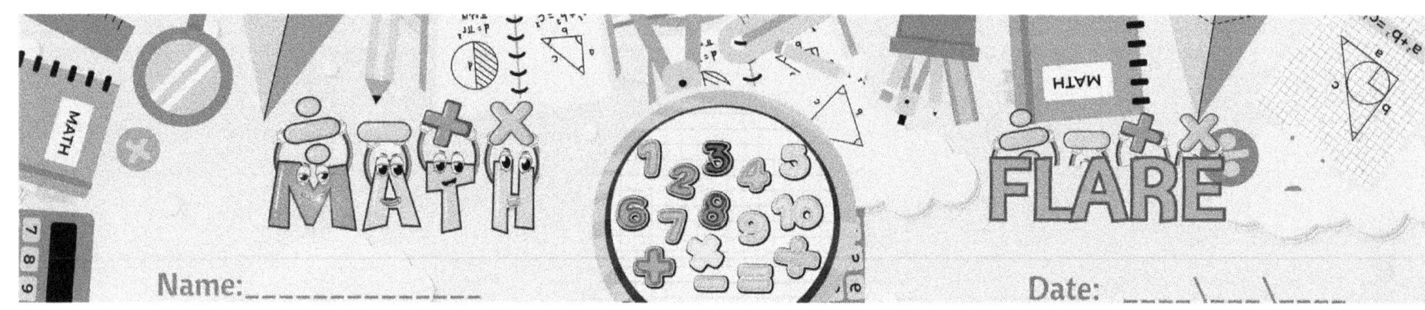

229.

$$7 \overline{)2,828}$$

230.

$$18 \overline{)7,132}$$

231.

$$12 \overline{)4,570}$$

232.

$$13 \overline{)5,085}$$

233.

$$17 \overline{)4,834}$$

234.

$$9 \overline{)6,760}$$

235.

$$19 \overline{)7{,}471}$$

236.

$$19 \overline{)8{,}585}$$

237.

$$18 \overline{)4{,}698}$$

238.

$$12 \overline{)1{,}372}$$

239.

$$12 \overline{)5{,}292}$$

240.

$$11 \overline{)1{,}977}$$

241.

11$\overline{)8,055}$

242.

12$\overline{)3,111}$

243.

12$\overline{)3,622}$

244.

12$\overline{)9,387}$

245.

17$\overline{)4,173}$

246.

15$\overline{)9,697}$

247.

$$18\overline{)2,028}$$

248.

$$6\overline{)5,502}$$

249.

$$11\overline{)8,029}$$

250.

$$3\overline{)7,405}$$

251.

$$13\overline{)9,778}$$

252.

$$8\overline{)1,351}$$

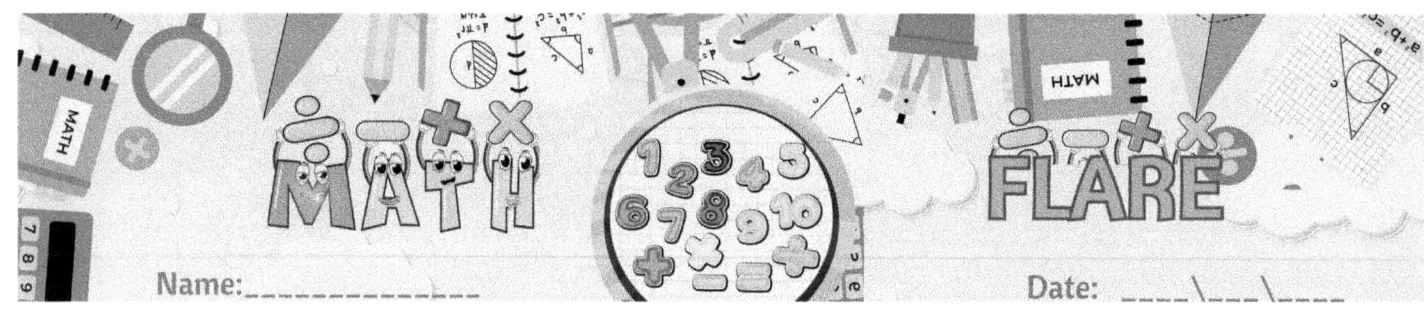

253.

$$17 \overline{)\ 1{,}368}$$

254.

$$9 \overline{)\ 7{,}350}$$

255.

$$7 \overline{)\ 8{,}024}$$

256.

$$14 \overline{)\ 2{,}093}$$

257.

$$5 \overline{)\ 2{,}749}$$

258.

$$18 \overline{)\ 1{,}942}$$

259.

$$18\overline{)4{,}112}$$

260.

$$17\overline{)4{,}088}$$

261.

$$4\overline{)9{,}076}$$

262.

$$18\overline{)1{,}268}$$

263.

$$4\overline{)9{,}894}$$

264.

$$11\overline{)8{,}540}$$

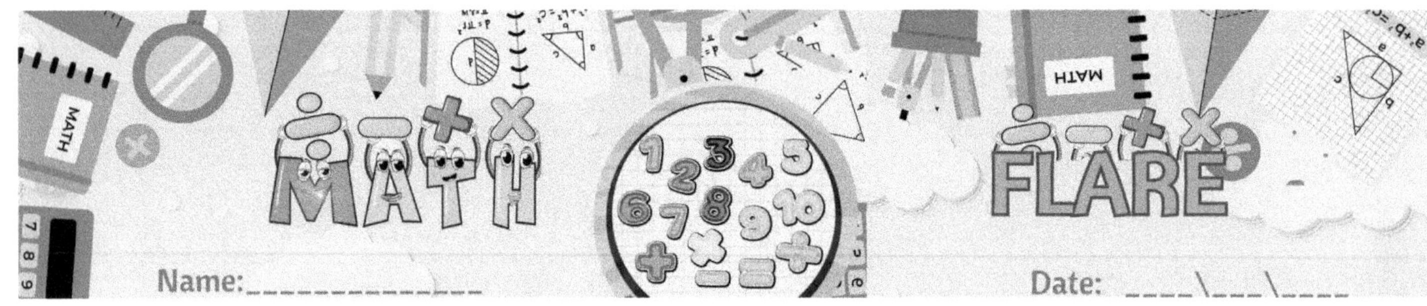

265.

$$17 \overline{)4{,}617}$$

266.

$$20 \overline{)7{,}995}$$

267.

$$3 \overline{)8{,}498}$$

268.

$$5 \overline{)5{,}642}$$

269.

$$19 \overline{)5{,}019}$$

270.

$$10 \overline{)5{,}526}$$

271.

$$12 \overline{)8{,}781}$$

272.

$$3 \overline{)7{,}913}$$

273.

$$8 \overline{)7{,}498}$$

274.

$$19 \overline{)5{,}765}$$

275.

$$13 \overline{)8{,}266}$$

276.

$$18 \overline{)8{,}774}$$

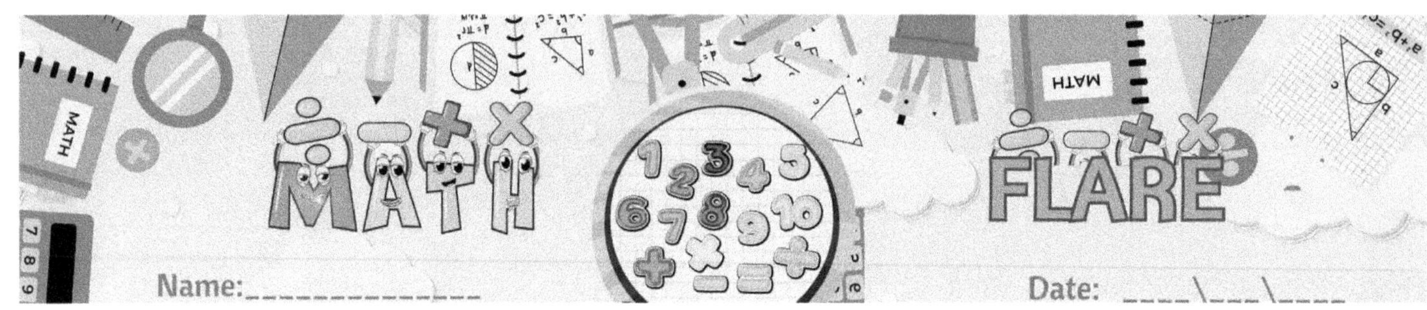

277.

$$17\overline{)2{,}323}$$

278.

$$18\overline{)2{,}306}$$

279.

$$5\overline{)6{,}089}$$

280.

$$19\overline{)3{,}938}$$

281.

$$6\overline{)9{,}977}$$

282.

$$19\overline{)9{,}677}$$

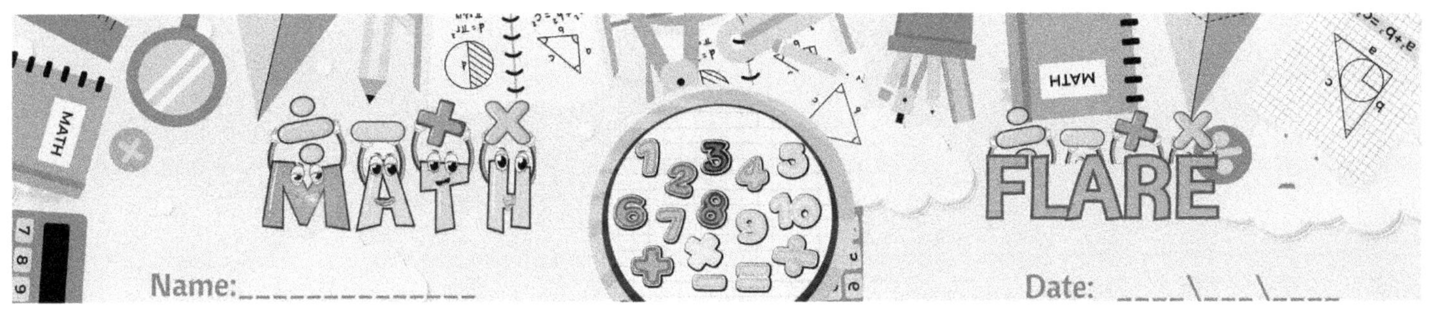

283.

$$4\overline{)5,584}$$

284.

$$4\overline{)8,425}$$

285.

$$18\overline{)7,068}$$

286.

$$10\overline{)5,180}$$

287.

$$18\overline{)4,664}$$

288.

$$8\overline{)9,918}$$

289.

$$19 \overline{)3{,}907}$$

290.

$$14 \overline{)2{,}382}$$

291.

$$18 \overline{)6{,}306}$$

292.

$$17 \overline{)7{,}223}$$

293.

$$18 \overline{)9{,}708}$$

294.

$$20 \overline{)8{,}558}$$

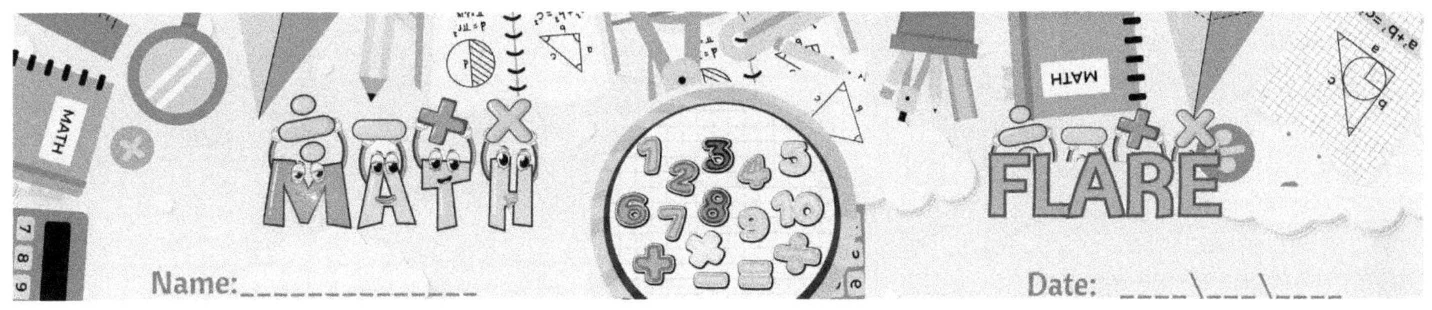

295.

$$13 \overline{)\,9{,}287}$$

296.

$$7 \overline{)\,6{,}606}$$

297.

$$12 \overline{)\,6{,}341}$$

298.

$$14 \overline{)\,5{,}125}$$

299.

$$17 \overline{)\,6{,}414}$$

300.

$$13 \overline{)\,6{,}008}$$

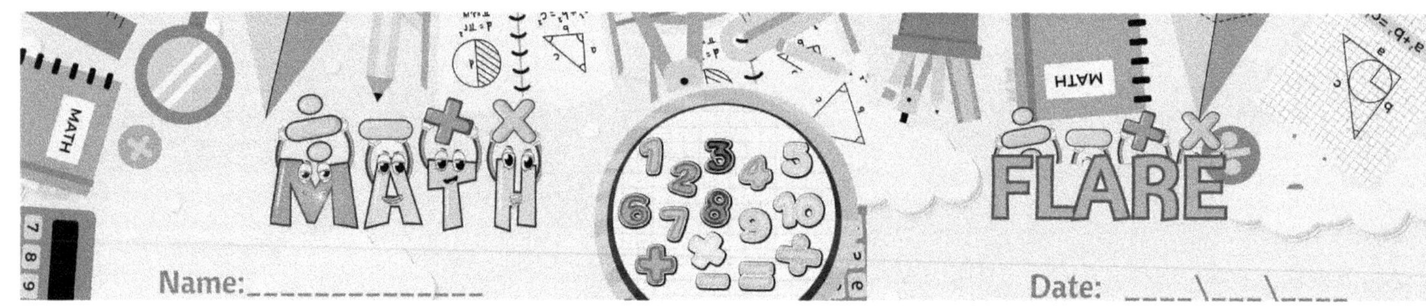

301.

$$9 \overline{)\ 5{,}347}$$

302.

$$18 \overline{)\ 3{,}249}$$

303.

$$10 \overline{)\ 2{,}122}$$

304.

$$7 \overline{)\ 5{,}175}$$

305.

$$17 \overline{)\ 8{,}784}$$

306.

$$13 \overline{)\ 6{,}050}$$

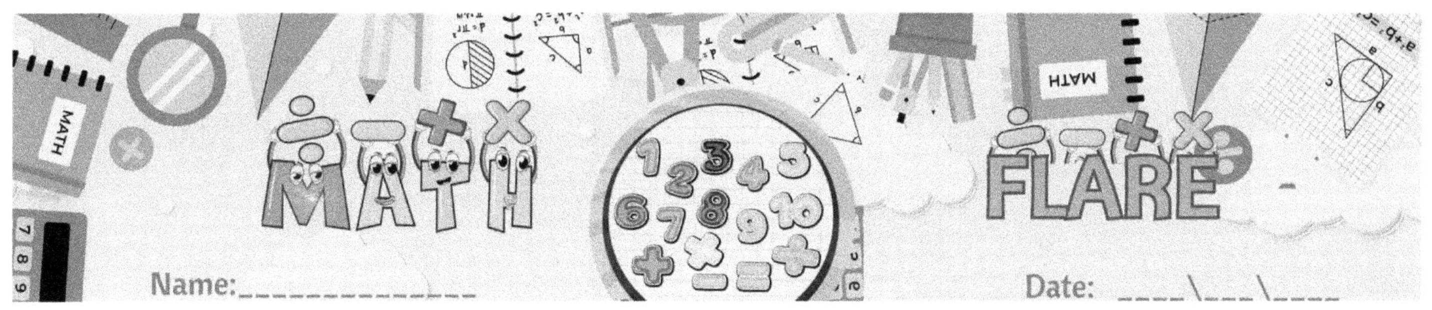

307.

$$14 \overline{)1{,}089}$$

308.

$$4 \overline{)3{,}990}$$

309.

$$5 \overline{)5{,}637}$$

310.

$$13 \overline{)9{,}830}$$

311.

$$17 \overline{)3{,}652}$$

312.

$$3 \overline{)2{,}866}$$

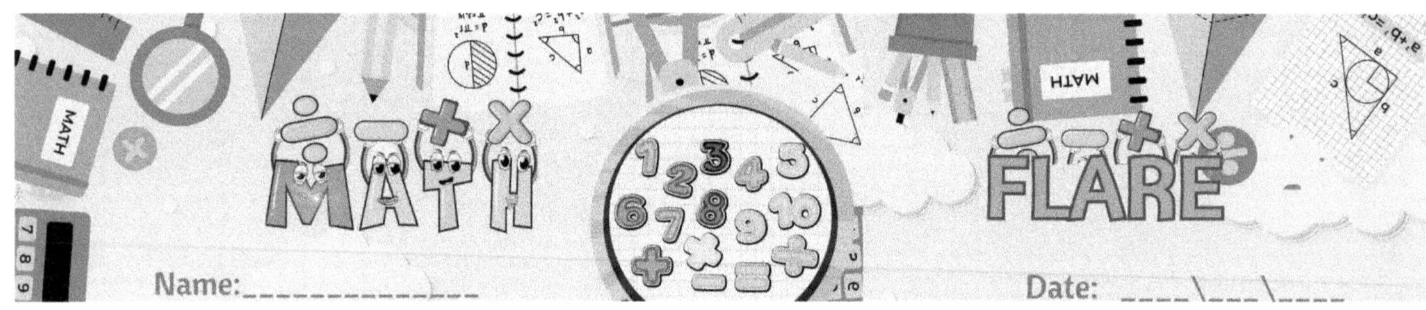

313.

$5 \overline{)3{,}638}$

314.

$17 \overline{)8{,}491}$

315.

$8 \overline{)4{,}859}$

316.

$11 \overline{)7{,}570}$

317.

$12 \overline{)4{,}666}$

318.

$5 \overline{)2{,}773}$

319.

$$16 \overline{)\,6{,}974}$$

320.

$$12 \overline{)\,7{,}192}$$

321.

$$12 \overline{)\,4{,}980}$$

322.

$$4 \overline{)\,2{,}010}$$

323.

$$2 \overline{)\,1{,}635}$$

324.

$$19 \overline{)\,3{,}458}$$

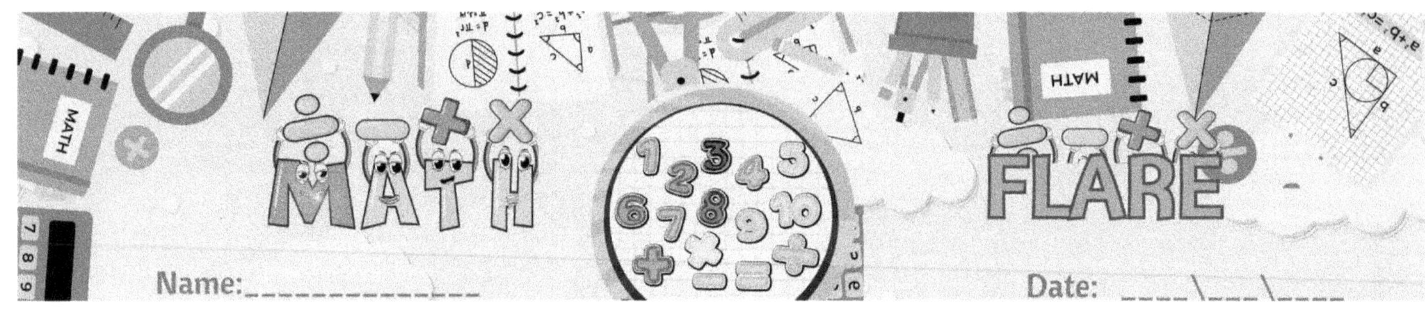

Name:________________   Date: ____________

Using the Power of 10

325.   7,000
      ×   100

326.   5,000
      × 1,000

327.   100)‾1,000

328.   2,000
      ×   10

329.   4,000
      ×   100

330.   100)‾7,000

331.   3,000
      × 1,000

332.   3,000
      × 1,000

333.   1,000)‾3,000

334.   100)‾5,000

335.   8,000
      × 1,000

336.   10)‾6,000

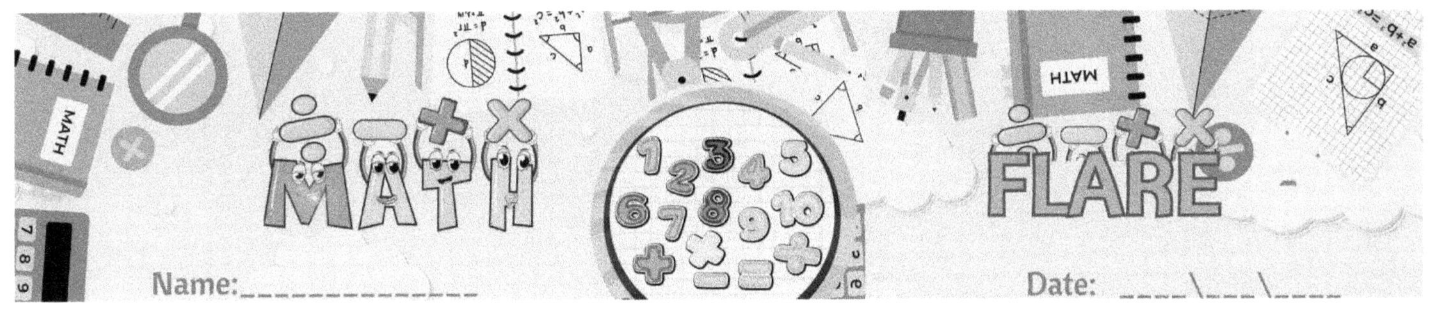

337. 8,000
    ×   100

338. 2,000
    × 1,000

339. 100) 9,000

340. 5,000
    ×   100

341. 5,000
    ×   100

342. 1,000) 5,000

343. 1,000
    ×   10

344. 100) 6,000

345. 1,000) 7,000

346. 1,000) 5,000

347. 10) 7,000

348. 8,000
    ×   100

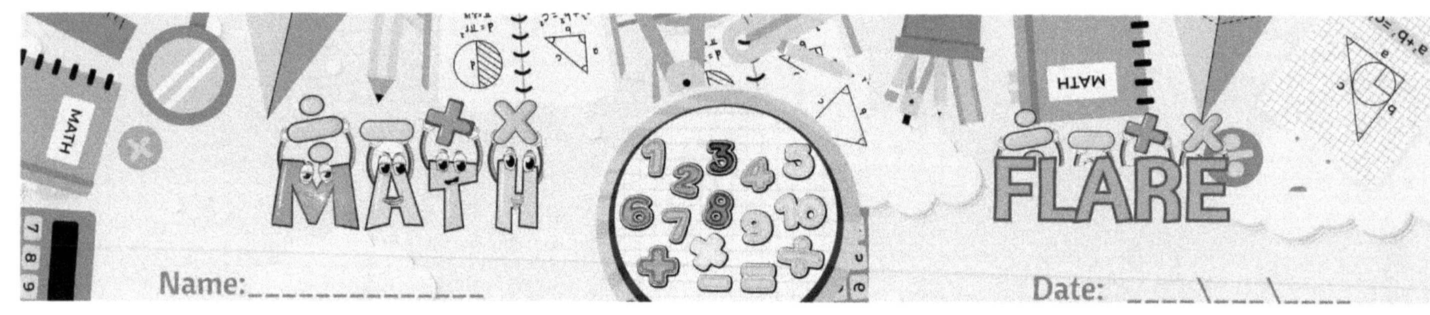

349.

$$10\overline{)4{,}000}$$

350.

$$100\overline{)3{,}000}$$

351.

$$\begin{array}{r} 4{,}000 \\ \times\ \ 1{,}000 \\ \hline \end{array}$$

352.

$$100\overline{)8{,}000}$$

353.

$$10\overline{)6{,}000}$$

354.

$$10\overline{)3{,}000}$$

355.

$$\begin{array}{r} 5{,}000 \\ \times\ \ \ \ 100 \\ \hline \end{array}$$

356.

$$10\overline{)5{,}000}$$

357.

$$\begin{array}{r} 7{,}000 \\ \times\ \ \ \ \ 10 \\ \hline \end{array}$$

358.

$$\begin{array}{r} 3{,}000 \\ \times\ \ \ \ 100 \\ \hline \end{array}$$

359.

$$1{,}000\overline{)2{,}000}$$

360.

$$10\overline{)8{,}000}$$

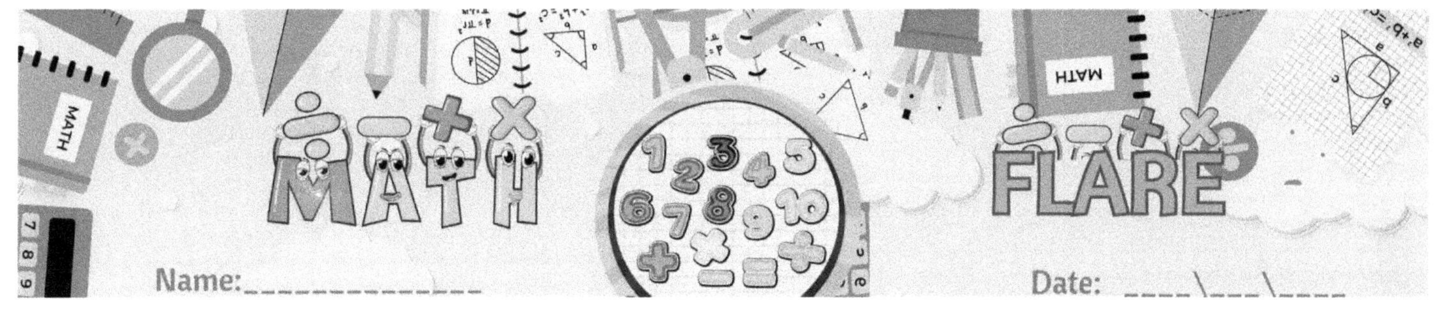

361.
$$4{,}000 \times 10$$

362.
$$10\overline{)3{,}000}$$

363.
$$1{,}000\overline{)4{,}000}$$

364.
$$100\overline{)8{,}000}$$

365.
$$8{,}000 \times 1{,}000$$

366.
$$6{,}000 \times 10$$

367.
$$100\overline{)7{,}000}$$

368.
$$8{,}000 \times 100$$

369.
$$4{,}000 \times 10$$

370.
$$5{,}000 \times 10$$

371.
$$1{,}000 \times 10$$

372.
$$7{,}000 \times 10$$

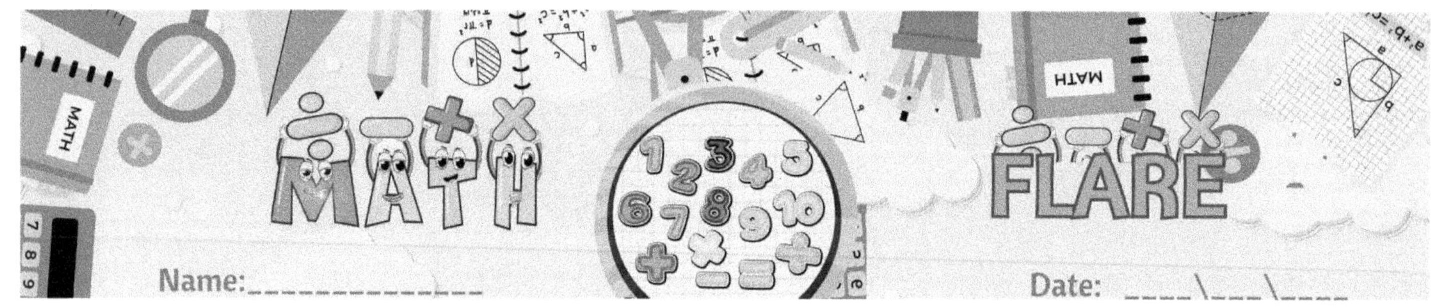

373.

$$10 \overline{)\ 1{,}000}$$

374.

$$100 \overline{)\ 5{,}000}$$

375.

$$10 \overline{)\ 2{,}000}$$

376.

$$\begin{array}{r} 3{,}000 \\ \times\ 1{,}000 \\ \hline \end{array}$$

377.

$$\begin{array}{r} 1{,}000 \\ \times\ 10 \\ \hline \end{array}$$

378.

$$1{,}000 \overline{)\ 7{,}000}$$

379.

$$\begin{array}{r} 9{,}000 \\ \times\ 100 \\ \hline \end{array}$$

380.

$$100 \overline{)\ 3{,}000}$$

381.

$$1{,}000 \overline{)\ 8{,}000}$$

382.

$$\begin{array}{r} 2{,}000 \\ \times\ 10 \\ \hline \end{array}$$

383.

$$1{,}000 \overline{)\ 8{,}000}$$

384.

$$\begin{array}{r} 1{,}000 \\ \times\ 1{,}000 \\ \hline \end{array}$$

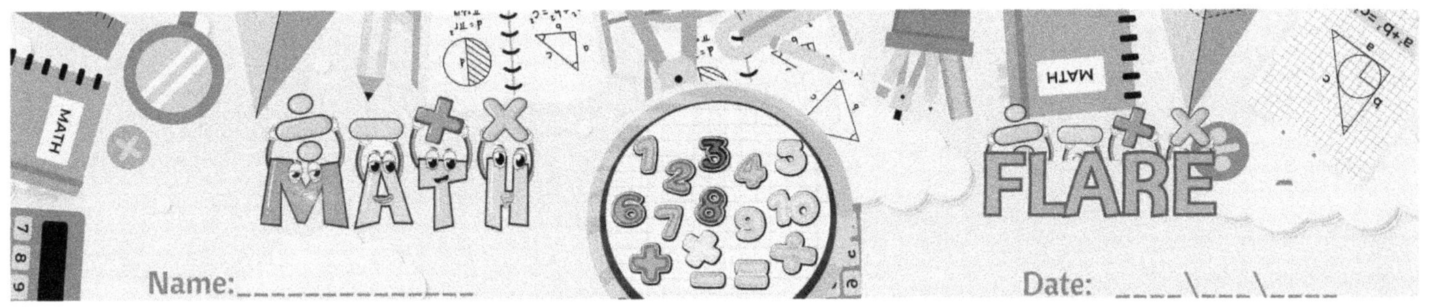

Multiplication Word Problems

385. Molly has seven jars of jam. Each jar has 18 ounces of jam. How many ounces of jam does Molly have in all?

386. Levi can type five words per minute. How many words can Levi type in 12 minutes?

387. Miles earns two dollars per hour. How much will Miles earn after working for 12 hours?

388. Charlotte baked two batches of cookies. Each batch had two cookies. How many cookies did Charlotte bake in all?

389. Lydia has two boxes of notebooks. Each box has 18 notebooks. How many notebooks does Lydia have in all?

390. Aubree baked 18 batches of cakes. Each batch had 15 cakes. How many cakes did Aubree bake in all?

391. Lucas can make 20 sandwiches in 1 hour. How many sandwiches can he make in 11 hour?

392. If there are six students in each classroom and there are nine classrooms, how many students are there in total?

393. There are 15 pencils in each pack. If Emma buys eight packs, how many pencils will Emma have?

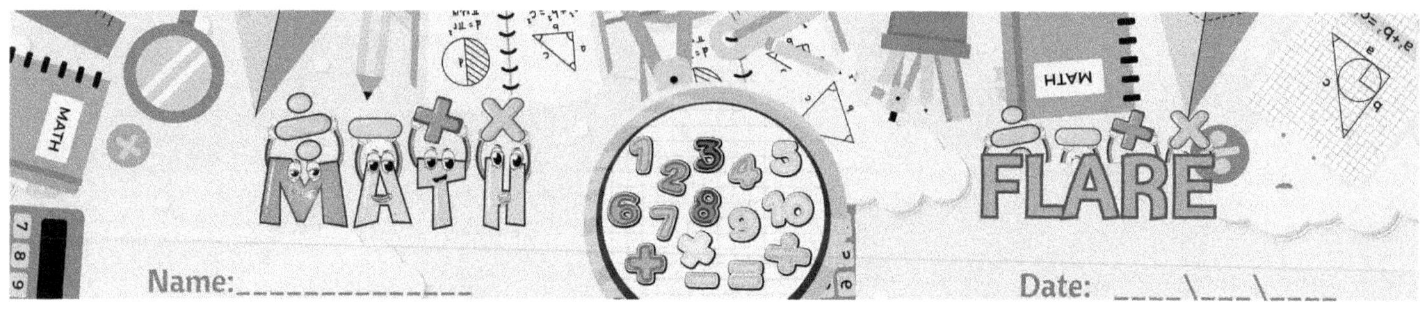

394. Nathaniel runs 18 miles every day. How many miles will Nathaniel run in 19 days?

395. If Liam can paint 14 square feet of wall in one hour, how many square feet of wall can he paint in seven hours?

396. If a boat travels at 14 miles per hour for 11 hours, how far will it go?

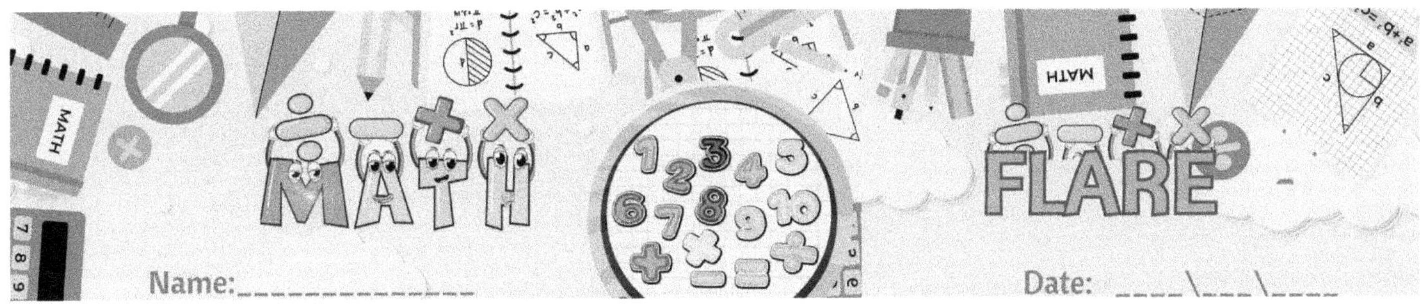

397. Ariana has 20 books. Each book has eight pages. How many pages does Ariana have in all?

398. There are 18 flowers in each bouquet. If Layla has 15 bouquets, how many flowers does Layla have in all?

399. A recipe for a cake calls for 19 cups of flour. How many cups of flour are needed to make 13 cakes?

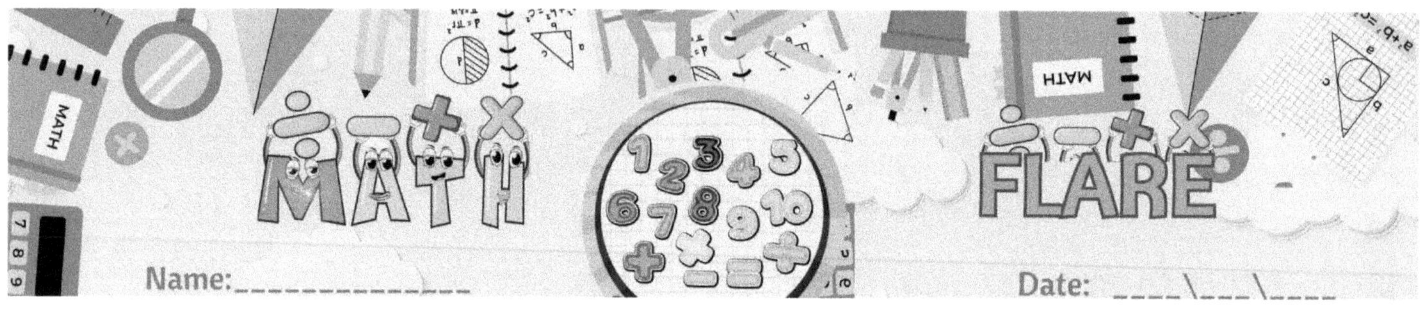

400. Aubrey has 15 vases of flowers. Each vase has 19 flowers. How many flowers does Aubrey have in all?

401. A movie theater can seat 16 people. How many people can it seat in six showings?

402. A garden has four rows of flowers and seven flowers in each row. How many flowers are there in total?

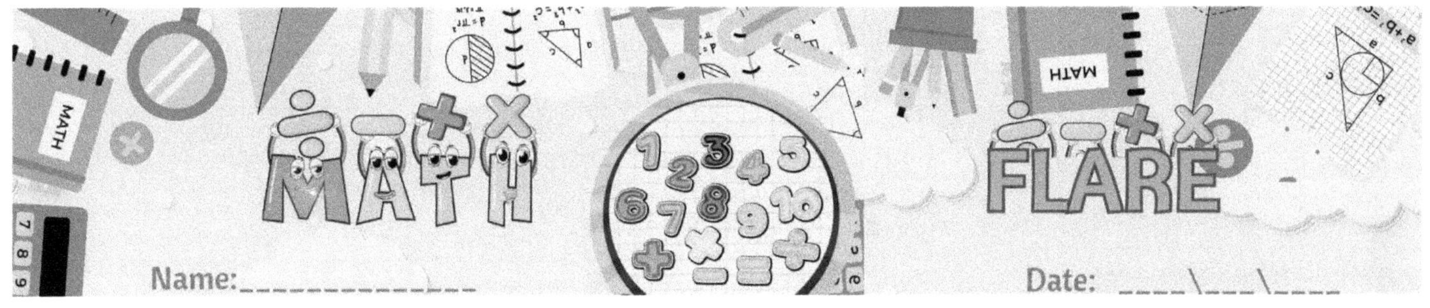

403. There are 11 cars in a parking lot. If each car needs 19 liters of gasoline, how many liters of gasoline are needed for all the cars?

404. Matthew runs 13 miles per week. How many miles will Matthew run in four weeks?

405. Grayson can lift 16 pounds of weight. How many pounds of weight can he lift in 18 repetitions?

406. Amelia wants to make 18 flower arrangements, and each arrangement requires 18 flowers. How many flowers does Amelia need in total?

407. A bookshelf can hold 10 books. If there are two bookshelves in a room, how many books can the room hold in total?

408. There are seven slices of pizza in each box. If Kinsley orders nine boxes, how many slices of pizza will Kinsley have?

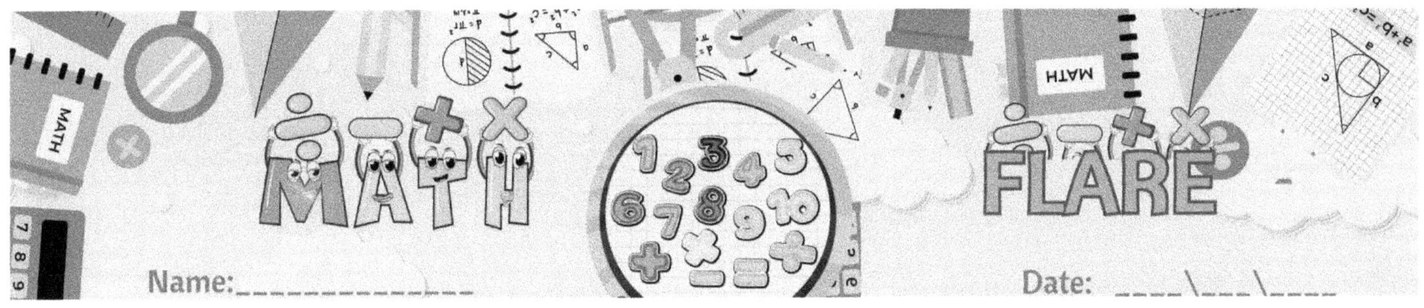

409. There are 18 medicines in each bag. If Camila buys six bags, how many medicines will Camila have?

410. There are 15 bananas in each bunch. If Luna buys 14 bunches, how many bananas will Luna have?

411. There are 20 students in a class. If each student needs five pencils, how many pencils are needed for the class in total?

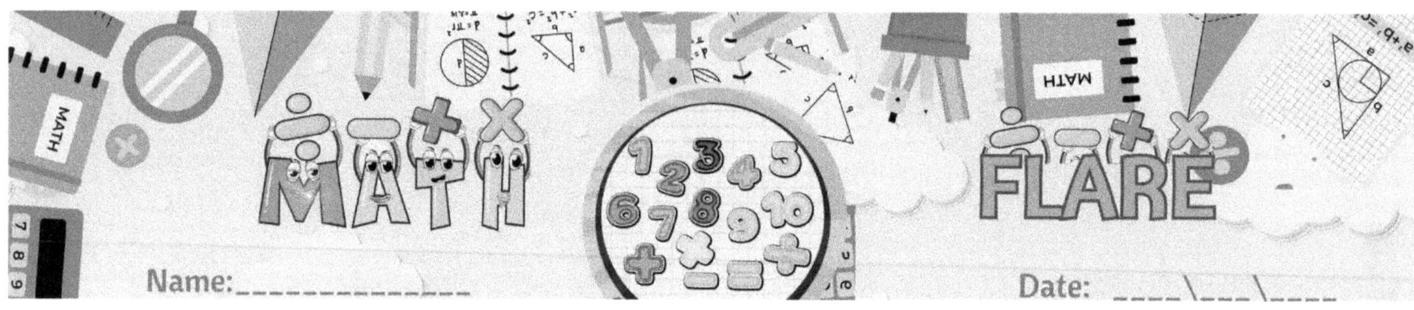

412. Henry sells eight cakes each day at his bakery. If he works 20 days, how many cakes does he sell?

413. Violet has five containers of paint. Each container holds 14 liters of paint. How many liters of paint does Violet have in total?

414. Micah can solve 12 math problems in one hour. How many problems can Micah solve in 14 hours?

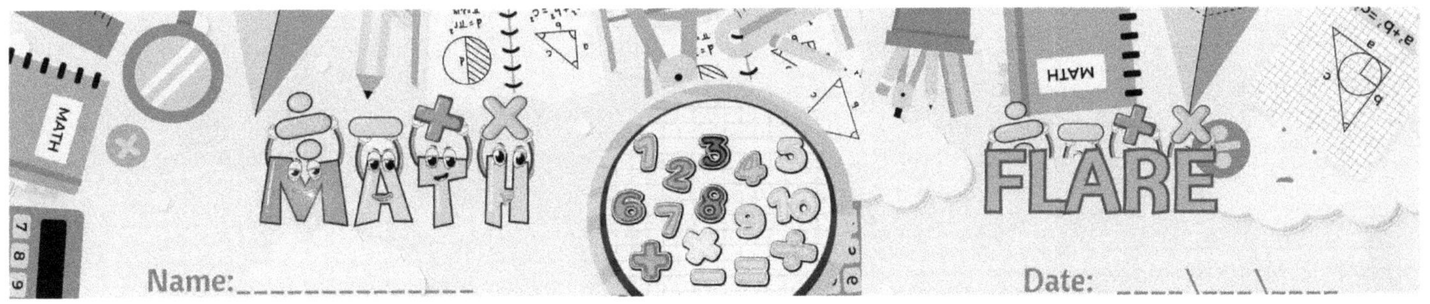

Division Word Problems

415. Parker drove 871 miles in 13 hours. What was Parker's average speed in miles per hour?

416. Trinity has 500 flowers and wants to divide them equally among five people. How many flowers will each person get?

417. If a box contains 39 globes and each person can have 13 globes, how many people can be served from that box?

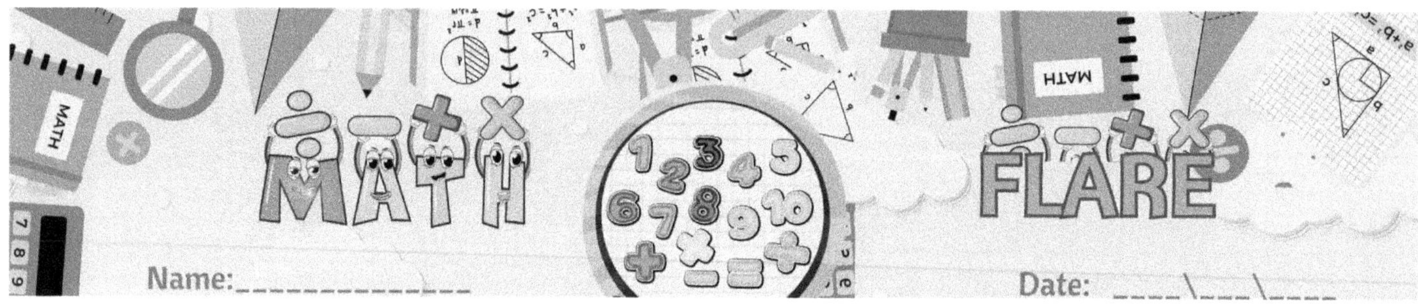

418. Luna has $966 and she wants to buy 14 gauzes that cost the same amount. How much does each gauzes cost?

419. A recipe calls for 759 cups of sugar to make 11 cookies. How much sugar is needed to make 1 cookie?

420. If a box contains 776 chocolates and each person can have eight chocolates, how many people can be served from that box?

421. A pool is 300 meters long. If it is divided into 12 equal parts, how long is each part?

422. A box contains 1,320 candy bars. If each candy bar has 20 calories, how many calories are there in the box?

423. Caleb scored 285 points in five games. What is his average score per game?

424. A book has 1,066 chapters. If you want to read the book in 13 days, how many chapters do you need to read per day?

425. If a store sells three pianos for $255 how much will each pianos cost?

426. If the pizzas have 460 slices and is divided equally among five people, how many slices will each person get?

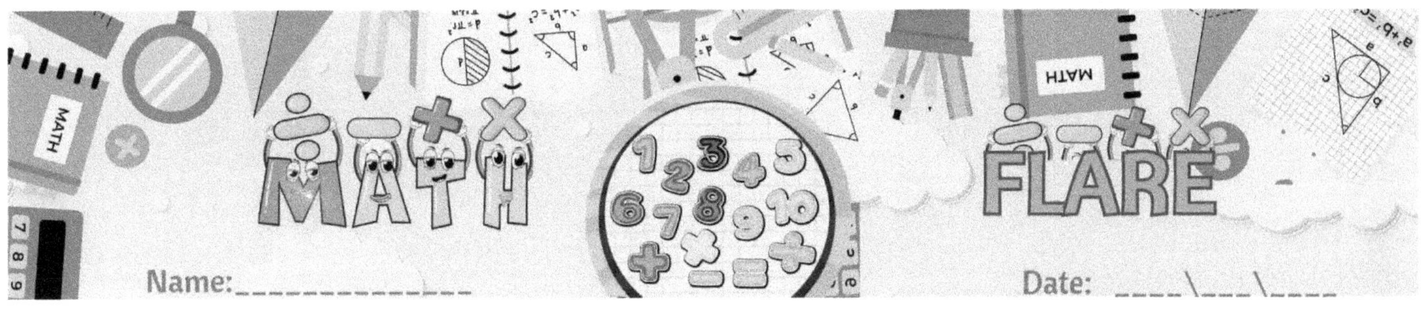

427. Isabella has 104 rulers. If Isabella divides them evenly among four children, how many rulers will each child get?

428. Stella has 1,598 pens and wants to divide them equally among 17 children. How many pens will each child get?

429. If a field is 228 acres and it is divided into four equal parts, how many acres is each part?

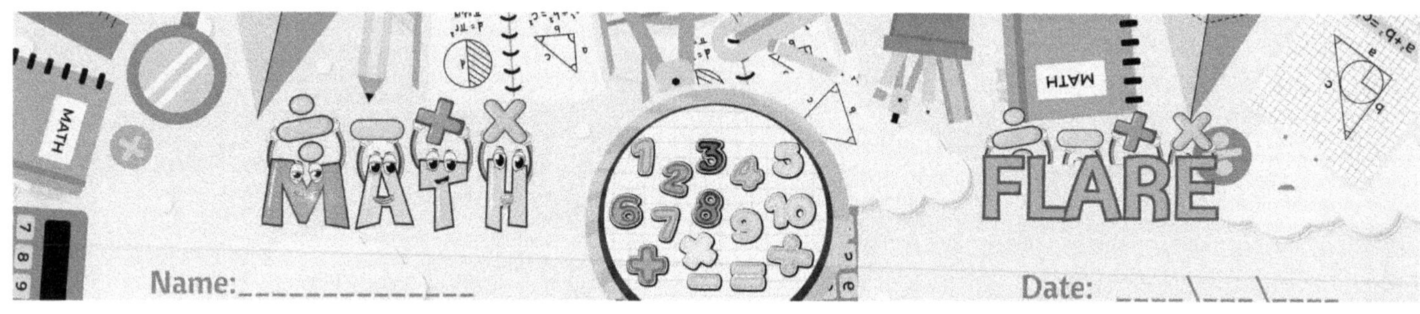

430. Christopher has 752 pages of homework to do. If he wants to finish his homework in 16 days, how many pages does he need to do each day?

431. Jaxon can type 602 words in 14 minutes. How many words can he type in 1 minute?

432. How many 18 cm pieces of rope can you cut from a rope that is 594 cm long?

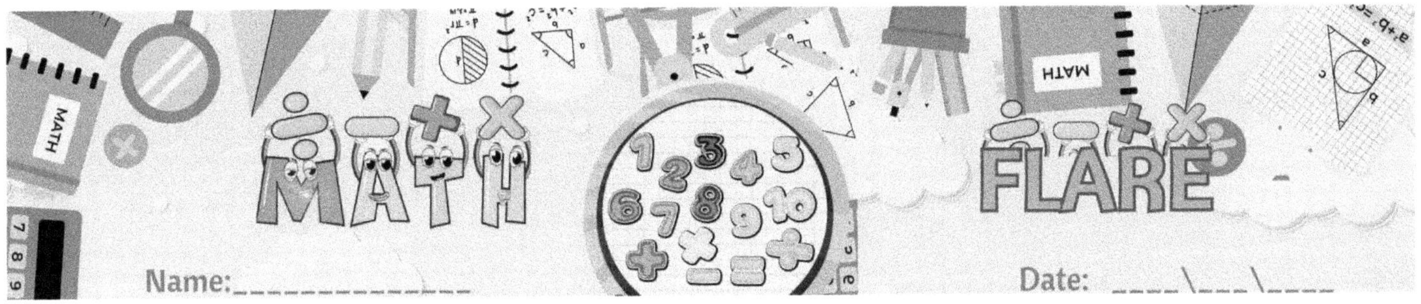

433. Reagan bought eight mirrors for a total of $760. How much did each mirrors cost?

434. Alice made 242 cookies for a bake sale. She put the cookies in bags, with 11 cookies in each bag. How many bags did she have for the bake sale?

435. If Carter has 312 radios and wants to share them equally among four friends, how many radios will each friend get?

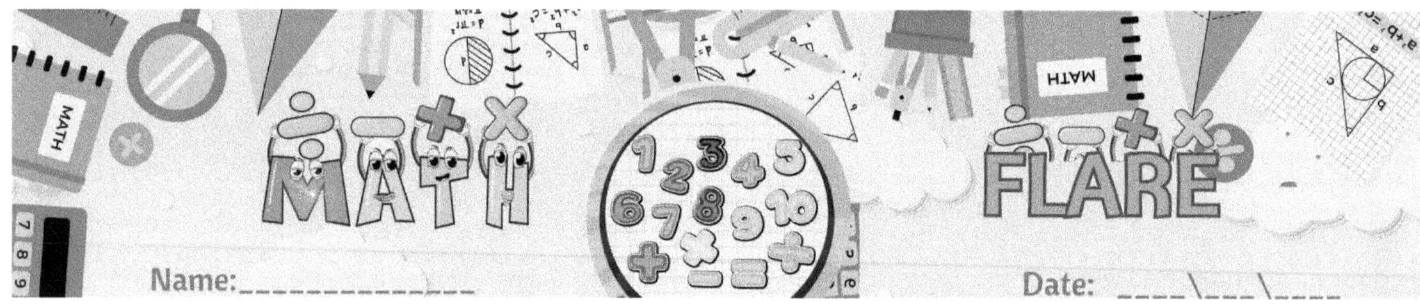

436. If a garden is 352 feet long and it is divided into four equal parts, how long is each part?

437. If Sadie has 686 pens and wants to distribute them equally to 14 students, how many pens will each student get?

438. Aubrey is packing 780 cupcakes into boxes. Each box can hold 15 cupcakes. How many boxes will Aubrey need?

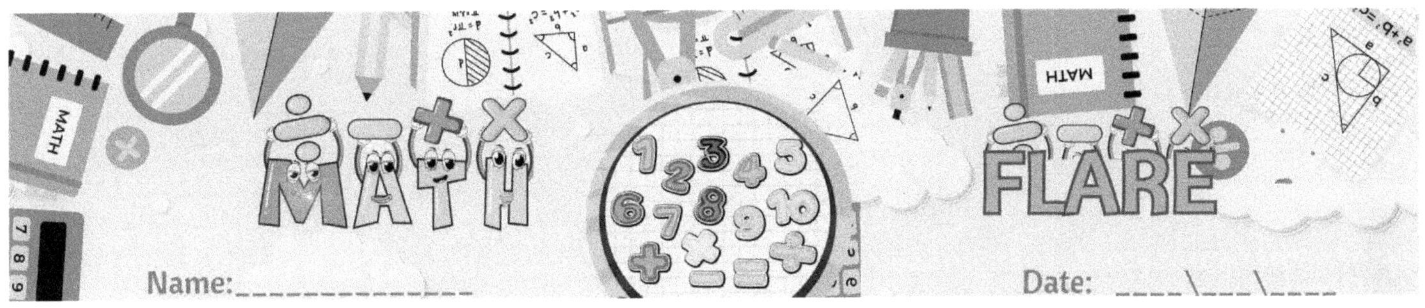

Name:_________________   Date: _____________

439. Adrian has 33 dollars and wants to buy three stethoscopes. How much can he spend on each stethoscopes?

440. Nolan is reading a book with 1,275 pages. If Nolan wants to read the same number of pages every day, how many pages would Nolan have to read each day to finish in 17 days?

441. How many 15 cm pieces of pipe can you cut from a pipe that is 1,485 cm long?

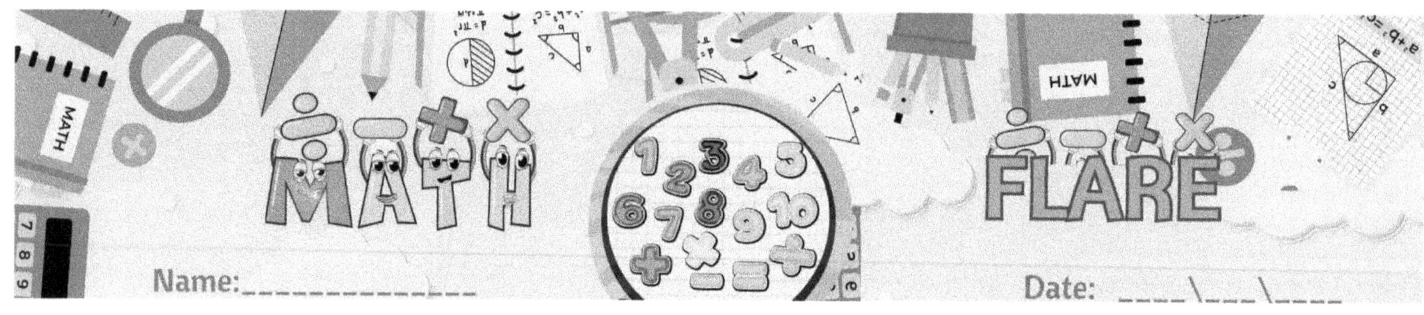

442. If a garden is 231 feet wide and it is divided into three equal parts, how wide is each part?

443. If Mila has 286 microphones and wants to distribute them equally to 11 students, how many microphones will each student get?

444. A car can travel 630 miles on 18 gallons of gas. How many miles can it travel on 1 gallon of gas?

ANSWERS

Page 1:   Multiplication: 4 x 1

1. 6,488   2. 2,622   3. 6,363   4. 6,428   5. 8,800   6. 1,931

7. 4,048   8. 6,339   9. 8,288   10. 9,069   11. 8,208   12. 3,063

13. 3,903   14. 2,424   15. 9,303   16. 8,084   17. 5,505   18. 6,485

19. 8,840   20. 6,330   21. 2,428   22. 6,399   23. 6,664   24. 3,966

25. 6,393   26. 9,366   27. 2,024   28. 8,666   29. 4,840   30. 9,465

31. 9,906   32. 5,550   33. 6,390   34. 8,088   35. 9,309   36. 8,044

37. 8,801   38. 8,848   39. 4,484   40. 4,846

Page 3:   Multiplication (double Digit)

41. 1,296   42. 324   43. 1,240   44. 2,150   45. 1,665

46. 2,968   47. 434   48. 1,428   49. 3,600   50. 870

51. 1,890   52. 714   53. 3,024   54. 1,106   55. 165

56. 1,530   57. 3,306   58. 3,069   59. 3,192   60. 2,278

61. 4,575   62. 6,975   63. 3,724   64. 2,214   65. 2,904

66. 2,496   67. 3,362   68. 588   69. 6,790   70. 5,796

71. 2,300   72. 1,344   73. 2,871   74. 6,256   75. 1,204

76. 493   77. 7,533   78. 6,806   79. 1,968   80. 7,826

81. 595   82. 3,102   83. 800   84. 1,380   85. 2,100

86. 544   87. 5,772   88. 3,198   89. 2,059   90. 2,280

91. 864   92. 3,950   93. 1,702   94. 2,700   95. 726

96. 5,928   97. 2,125   98. 7,524   99. 7,544   100. 2,368

101. 3,551   102. 693   103. 1,450   104. 5,141   105. 4,864

106. 4,615   107. 5,304   108. 5,628   109. 546   110. 2,940

111. 255   112. 3,770   113. 456   114. 5,896   115. 2,028

116. 7,216

Page 8: Multiplication (3 Digit)

117. 497,408   118. 776,020   119. 94,120   120. 257,012

121. 346,580   122. 221,835   123. 18,306   124. 269,652

125. 170,469   126. 373,038   127. 308,425   128. 359,900

129. 932,900   130. 348,244   131. 161,600   132. 53,703

133. 725,063   134. 278,432   135. 774,384   136. 66,560

137. 95,764   138. 474,192   139. 179,912   140. 206,724

141. 101,673   142. 363,750   143. 29,850   144. 590,108

145. 278,775   146. 31,464   147. 368,823   148. 273,972

149. 217,568   150. 133,518   151. 268,250   152. 206,682

153. 404,950   154. 557,983   155. 248,253   156. 132,022

157. 220,314   158. 301,344   159. 35,088   160. 133,893

161. 259,347   162. 276,486   163. 292,320   164. 294,216

165. 390,696   166. 27,600   167. 400,400   168. 396,567

169. 353,115   170. 112,640   171. 398,696   172. 785,063

173. 84,249   174. 195,858   175. 67,239   176. 70,028

177. 306,229   178. 538,764   179. 300,004   180. 436,752

181. 200,872   182. 144,088   183. 153,714   184. 810,150

185. 66,671   186. 102,375   187. 98,792   188. 197,895

189. 450,214   190. 323,162   191. 178,284   192. 224,878

193. 52,007   194. 195,048   195. 240,075   196. 692,220

197. 149,072   198. 283,127   199. 185,235   200. 27,000

201. 496,174   202. 150,040   203. 103,845   204. 129,888

205. 218,112   206. 548,160   207. 44,770   208. 192,238

209. 545,952   210. 289,930   211. 336,336   212. 93,132

213. 84,196   214. 700,828   215. 83,538   216. 655,218

217. 184,482   218. 630,783   219. 228,150   220. 224,234

221. 661,674   222. 839,056   223. 125,528   224. 123,319

Page 17:   Long Division: Remainders

225. 190 R5   226. 2,022 R0   227. 200 R15   228. 662 R0

229. 404 R0   230. 396 R4   231. 380 R10   232. 391 R2

233. 284 R6   234. 751 R1   235. 393 R4   236. 451 R16

237. 261 R0   238. 114 R4   239. 441 R0   240. 179 R8

241. 732 R3   242. 259 R3   243. 301 R10   244. 782 R3

245. 245 R8   246. 646 R7   247. 112 R12   248. 917 R0

249. 729 R10   250. 2,468 R1   251. 752 R2   252. 168 R7

253. 80 R8   254. 816 R6   255. 1,146 R2   256. 149 R7

257. 549 R4   258. 107 R16   259. 228 R8   260. 240 R8

261. 2,269 R0   262. 70 R8   263. 2,473 R2   264. 776 R4

265. 271 R10   266. 399 R15   267. 2,832 R2   268. 1,128 R2

269. 264 R3   270. 552 R6   271. 731 R9   272. 2,637 R2

273. 937 R2   274. 303 R8   275. 635 R11   276. 487 R8

277. 136 R11   278. 128 R2   279. 1,217 R4   280. 207 R5

281. 1,662 R5   282. 509 R6   283. 1,396 R0   284. 2,106 R1

285. 392 R12   286. 518 R0   287. 259 R2   288. 1,239 R6

289. 205 R12   290. 170 R2   291. 350 R6   292. 424 R15

293. 539 R6   294. 427 R18   295. 714 R5   296. 943 R5

297. 528 R5   298. 366 R1   299. 377 R5   300. 462 R2

301. 594 R1   302. 180 R9   303. 212 R2   304. 739 R2

305. 516 R12   306. 465 R5   307. 77 R11   308. 997 R2

309. 1,127 R2   310. 756 R2   311. 214 R14   312. 955 R1

313. 727 R3   314. 499 R8   315. 607 R3   316. 688 R2

317. 388 R10   318. 554 R3   319. 435 R14   320. 599 R4

321. 415 R0   322. 502 R2   323. 817 R1   324. 182 R0

Page 34:   Using the Power of 10

325. 700,000   326. 5,000,000   327. 10   328. 20,000

329. 400,000   330. 70   331. 3,000,000   332. 3,000,000

333. 3   334. 50   335. 8,000,000   336. 600

337. 800,000   338. 2,000,000   339. 90   340. 500,000

341. 500,000   342. 5   343. 10,000   344. 60

345. 7   346. 5   347. 700   348. 800,000

349. 400   350. 30   351. 4,000,000   352. 80

353. 600   354. 300   355. 500,000   356. 500

357. 70,000   358. 300,000   359. 2   360. 800

361. 40,000   362. 300   363. 4   364. 80

365. 8,000,000   366. 60,000   367. 70   368. 800,000

369. 40,000   370. 50,000   371. 10,000   372. 70,000

373. 100   374. 50   375. 200   376. 3,000,000

377. 10,000   378. 7   379. 900,000   380. 30

381. 8   382. 20,000   383. 8   384. 1,000,000

Page 39: Multiplication Word Problems

385. 126   386. 60   387. 24   388. 4   389. 36   390. 270

391. 220   392. 54   393. 120   394. 342   395. 98   396. 154

397. 160   398. 270   399. 247   400. 285   401. 96   402. 28

403. 209   404. 52   405. 288   406. 324   407. 20   408. 63

409. 108   410. 210   411. 100   412. 160   413. 70   414. 168

Page 49: Division Word Problems

415. 67   416. 100   417. 3   418. 69   419. 69   420. 97   421. 25

422. 66   423. 57   424. 82   425. 85   426. 92   427. 26   428. 94

429. 57   430. 47   431. 43   432. 33   433. 95   434. 22   435. 78

436. 88   437. 49   438. 52   439. 11   440. 75   441. 99   442. 77

443. 26   444. 35

www.ingramcontent.com/pod-product-compliance
Lightning Source LLC
Chambersburg PA
CBHW041836110726
48006CB00020B/2642